OECD Economic Surveys: Portugal 2012

This document and any map included herein are without prejudice to the status of or sovereignty over any territory, to the delimitation of international frontiers and boundaries and to the name of any territory, city or area.

Please cite this publication as:
OECD (2012), *OECD Economic Surveys: Portugal 2012*, OECD Publishing.
http://dx.doi.org/10.1787/eco_surveys-prt-2012-en

ISBN 978-92-64-12798-2 (print)
ISBN 978-92-64-12799-9 (PDF)

Series: OECD Economic Surveys
ISSN 0376-6438 (print)
ISSN 1609-7513 (online)

OECD Economic Surveys Country: Portugal
ISSN 1995-3348 (print)
ISSN 1999-0405 (online)

The statistical data for Israel are supplied by and under the responsibility of the relevant Israeli authorities. The use of such data by the OECD is without prejudice to the status of the Golan Heights, East Jerusalem and Israeli settlements in the West Bank under the terms of international law.

Photo credits: Cover © Comstock/Comstock Images/Getty Images.

Corrigenda to OECD publications may be found on line at: *www.oecd.org/publishing/corrigenda*.
© OECD 2012

You can copy, download or print OECD content for your own use, and you can include excerpts from OECD publications, databases and multimedia products in your own documents, presentations, blogs, websites and teaching materials, provided that suitable acknowledgment of OECD as source and copyright owner is given. All requests for public or commercial use and translation rights should be submitted to *rights@oecd.org*. Requests for permission to photocopy portions of this material for public or commercial use shall be addressed directly to the Copyright Clearance Center (CCC) at *info@copyright.com* or the Centre français d'exploitation du droit de copie (CFC) at *contact@cfcopies.com*.

Table of contents

Executive summary 8

Key recommendations 10

Assessment and recommendations 11
    Challenges facing Portugal 11
    Financial stability 16
    Fiscal policy 20
    Education, labour and social policies............................. 28
    Progress in improving the business environment and product markets 34
    Bibliography... 42

    Annex A1. Progress in main structural reforms 45

Chapter 1. **Solid foundations for a sustainable fiscal consolidation** 47
    Introduction... 48
    The consolidation programme: how fast and with which instruments?......... 48
    Improving the fiscal framework 52
    Public sector efficiency and off-balance sheet liabilities 60

    Notes.. 77
    Bibliography... 77

    Annex 1.A1. Sensitivity of stochastic simulation results 80

Chapter 2. **Rebalancing the economy and returning to growth through job creation and better capital allocation** 83
    The crisis made imbalances unsustainable 84
    Unwinding macro-financial imbalances............................. 88
    Removing distortions to investment allocation 94
    Reforming the labour market to create jobs and help rebalance the economy.... 101
    Bibliography.. 111

Glossary 115

Boxes
    1. The EU-IMF Adjustment Programme................................ 11
    2. Core recommendations on financial stability 19
    3. Core recommendations to improve fiscal performance............. 28
    4. Core recommendations to improve education, labour market and social cohesion 34
    5. Core recommendations on the business environment and product markets... 42
    1.1. The structure of Portuguese subnational government.......... 68

TABLE OF CONTENTS

- 1.2. The financial assistance plan to Madeira 69
- 1.3. Municipalities have cyclical resources and little fiscal autonomy 72
- 1.4. EU structural and cohesion funds in Portugal 74
- 1.5. Summary of recommendations for restoring fiscal sustainability and lifting public sector efficiency 76
- 2.1. Support to electricity generators 98
- 2.2. The Programme for PES Reform 108
- 2.3. Summary of recommendations to rebalance the economy and return to growth 110

Tables

1. Short-term outlook 14
2. General government revenue and expenditure 20
3. Stability Programme targets and assumptions 21
1.1. Stability programme targets and assumptions 49
1.2. Road sector public-private partnership models 65
2.1. Data on bank recapitalisation for the eight largest groups 89
2.2. Spending on active labour market programmes 108

Figures

1. Key indicators 13
2. Potential growth 15
3. Banking sector indicators 18
4. Loans of financial institutions to households and non-financial corporations. 19
5. Fiscal consolidation in international comparison 21
6. Assessing the risks around the fiscal consolidation programme 22
7. Forecasts for general government net lending and expenditure 23
8. State-owned enterprise performance 25
9. Inequality and level of educational attainment 29
10. Unemployment developments over the past decade 30
11. Strictness of employment protection legislation 32
12. Duration of unemployment benefits 33
13. Productivity growth by sector 35
14. Greenhouse gas emissions 38
15. Evolution of electricity prices 39
16. Gas prices in international comparison 40
17. Mobile telephone prices in international comparison 41
1.1. Long-run fiscal indicators 48
1.2. Stochastic simulation results 50
1.3. Fiscal policy phases and breakdown of current expenditure 53
1.4. Forecast errors for real GDP and general government revenue 54
1.5. Expenditure growth forecast errors 55
1.6. Employment in state-owned enterprises 60
1.7. State-owned enterprise performance 61
1.8. Rail infrastructure access charges 63
1.9. Public-private partnership contracts reaching financial close 64
1.10. Net public-private partnership payments by the government 66

1.11.	Indicator of efficiency constraining features of public-private partnership frameworks.	67
1.12.	Local government revenue and expenditure	68
1.13.	Local government debt	69
1.14.	Local government tax revenue in Portugal	72
1.15.	Absorption of EU structural and cohesion funds by end 2011	74
1.A1.1.	Sensitivity analysis: Fiscal multiplier of 0.5 (instead of 1)	80
1.A1.2.	Sensitivity analysis: Average potential growth over 2012-16 of +1% (instead of +0.3%)	81
2.1.	Financial debt	85
2.2.	Private consumption and gross fixed capital formation	85
2.3.	Developments in cost competitiveness	86
2.4.	Investment allocation by assets and sectors	87
2.5.	Banking sector developments	87
2.6.	Recent developments in banks' loan-to-deposit ratio	90
2.7.	Credit to non-financial firms	91
2.8.	Provision of Eurosystem liquidity to Portuguese banks	92
2.9.	Housing structure in international comparison	94
2.10.	Share of renewables in electricity production	97
2.11.	Unit revenue paid to electricity generators	99
2.12.	Average electricity price structure	99
2.13.	Strictness of employment protection legislation	105
2.14.	Ratio of unemployment benefit recipients to the number of unemployed	107

This Survey is published on the responsibility of the Economic and Development Review Committee of the OECD, which is charged with the examination of the economic situation of member countries.

The economic situation and policies of Portugal were reviewed by the Committee on 3 July 2012. The draft report was then revised in the light of the discussions and given final approval as the agreed report of the whole Committee on 16 July 2012.

The Secretariat's draft report was prepared for the Committee by David Haugh, Álvaro Pina, Stéphane Sorbe and Ildeberta Abreu under the supervision of Pierre Beynet. Statistical assistance was provided by Desney Erb.

The previous Survey of Portugal was issued in September 2010.

This book has...

StatLinks

A service that delivers Excel® files from the printed page!

Look for the *StatLinks* at the bottom right-hand corner of the tables or graphs in this book. To download the matching Excel® spreadsheet, just type the link into your Internet browser, starting with the *http://dx.doi.org* prefix.
If you're reading the PDF e-book edition, and your PC is connected to the Internet, simply click on the link. You'll find *StatLinks* appearing in more OECD books.

BASIC STATISTICS OF PORTUGAL, 2011

LAND (2010)

Total area (1 000 km²)	92.2	Major cities, resident population (thousand)	
Agriculture (% of total)	39.9	Greater Lisbon	2 035
		Greater Porto	1 286

PEOPLE

Population		Total labour force (thousands)	5 513
Thousands	10 562	Employment (% of total)	
Increase 2006-11 (annual rate, %)	–0.04	Agriculture, forestry and fishing	10.0
Number of inhabitants per km²	115	Industry, construction, energy and water	27.5
		Services	62.5

PRODUCTION

Gross domestic product		Gross fixed capital investment	
In billion euros	171	In % of GDP	18.1
Per head (thousand USD)	22.5	Per head (thousand USD)	4.1

GOVERNMENT

Public consumption (% of GDP)	20.1	Number of seats in Parliament	230
General government (% of GDP)		Social Democratic Party (PSD)	108
Current expenditure	47.4	Socialist Party (PS)	74
Current revenue	40.3	People's Party (CDS/PP)	24
Gross debt, Maastricht definition	107.8	Democratic Unity Coalition (CDU)	16
		Left Block (BE)	8
		Last general elections: June 2011	

FOREIGN TRADE

Exports of goods and services (% of GDP)	35.5	Imports of goods and services (% of GDP)	39.3
Main commodity exports (% of total)		Main commodity imports (% of total)	
Industrial supplies	35.7	Industrial supplies	28.7
Transport equipment	18.4	Fuels and lubricants	17.3
Consumer goods	18.3	Consumer goods	14.7

CURRENCY

Monetary unit: euro	Currency units per US dollar, average of daily figures
	Year 2011 0.719
	June 2012 0.798

Executive summary

Portugal has started down a long road of economic adjustment to boost growth and correct an excessive reliance on debt. The government is resolutely implementing the EU-IMF financial assistance programme of fiscal adjustment and reform. Accordingly, significant legislation has been passed, with broad political support, to improve the performance of the labour and product markets. In addition, many OECD recommendations of the last survey have been adopted. The authorities should ensure effective implementation of these ambitious reforms. Returning to a sustainable fiscal position is a pre-condition for restoring confidence, investment and growth. The authorities should therefore aim to meet the headline deficit targets in the EU-IMF programme. However, the government may need to let automatic stabilisers play at least partially if risks materialise and growth turns out much lower than projected in the programme, while sticking to its structural fiscal targets to restore investors' confidence. At the same time, credit to the economy should be supported by promoting swift recognition of bad loans, and ensuring that the banks maintain the required capital ratios and the pace of convergence towards the indicative target for the loan-to-deposit ratio does not thwart economic activity. Special attention should be paid to the financing conditions of small and medium-sized enterprises, notably by making firms more reliant on equity and less on debt, and by re-directing EU funds. Fundamental structural reforms are central to boosting potential growth and shifting economic activity from low-productivity domestically-orientated sectors to tradable goods and services. Vigorous reforms of the labour market would combat duality and boost competitiveness.

Structural fiscal reforms are required to return to fiscal sustainability. Still-high bond spreads indicate that the government faces additional challenges to regain full market access within the programme period. Structural measures are required to tackle a long history of excessive spending growth and substantial liabilities that have been built up non-transparently through payment arrears, state owned company losses and public-private partnerships. The introduction by the government of a medium-term budget framework, better financial management tools, a fiscal council and greater transparency in fiscal accounts are welcome. In addition, the fiscal framework would be significantly reinforced by introducing a clear, operational expenditure rule for general government, in line with the new European fiscal framework. Local and regional government finances have generated large negative surprises and reforms to their fiscal frameworks are also required, as envisaged.

A wide range of structural reforms is required to raise productivity and rebalance the economy towards international trade. Although legally liberalised, many markets remain concentrated due to significant barriers to entry, hampering competition and innovation. Streamlining business licensing procedures, as planned, would encourage firm entry, competition and employment. Portugal's international trade is limited, considering the relatively small size of its economy, pointing to potential gains from increased participation in global value chains. It is important that the government follows through on efforts to improve the business environment, including in the markets concerned by privatisations, and reduces distorting incentives that have biased investment away from the tradable sector. This will help to attract foreign direct investment. Education levels in the workforce are still far below the European average and need to improve further, despite the significant progress in the younger generation, to enable firms to expand into more productive activities.

Further reforms of the labour market are necessary. Institutional settings have stifled employment and generated a dualistic labour market that undermines productivity growth, as workers with short-term contracts are less likely to invest in human capital and those with permanent contracts have insufficient mobility. Efforts are going in the right direction to reduce duality, with significant reforms legislated recently, such as the reduction of severance payments, following an agreement with social partners. However, dominant firms impose wage and working conditions on others via the administrative extension of collective agreements, reducing competition and entry, thereby hurting competitiveness. Dualism would be further eased by reducing severance pay and tackling delays and uncertainty in litigation over dismissals. Finally, cutting non-wage costs for the low-paid could help boost employment prospects of the less qualified.

Key recommendations

Macroeconomic policies to stabilise the economy

- The government should aim to meet headline deficit targets in the programme, notably through abiding by the budgeted expenditure at all levels of general government. If risks materialise significantly and growth is far lower than projected in the programme, the automatic stabilisers could be allowed to operate at least partially.
- Introduce an explicit and easily enforceable public expenditure rule consistent with revenue projections and medium-term fiscal objectives and in line with the European fiscal framework.
- Support to local and regional governments should be accompanied with improvements in the fiscal framework.
- Pay special attention to financing conditions of small and medium-sized enterprises, notably by making firms more reliant on equity and by re-directing EU funds.
- Ensure that the pace of convergence towards the indicative target for the loan-to-deposit ratio does not thwart economic activity.

Structural policies to rebalance the economy and boost growth

- Maintain the momentum in justice reform to speed up civil and commercial case resolution.
- Fully implement the proposed zero authorisation initiative to speed up local licensing.
- Ensure that electricity generation support is made cost-effective and costs are fully passed on to all consumers. This requires further reducing excessive support to both wind farms and cogeneration, and to fossil-fuel power and large hydro plants.
- Further reduce severance pay and introduce binding arbitration in conflicts over dismissals.
- Further promote firm-level wage bargaining by abolishing administrative extension of collective agreements.
- Lift education levels by focusing the evaluation system more on tracking individuals and cohorts over time in order to inform policy changes to improve education outcomes of children from lower socio-economic backgrounds.

Assessment and recommendations

Challenges facing Portugal

The global crisis exposed underlying weaknesses and imbalances in the Portuguese economy, which has entered a deep recession with high unemployment. Labour market regulation had long been ill-equipped to create jobs and wide-ranging structural reforms were needed to help get the unemployed back to work and foster reallocation of labour from non-tradable to tradable sectors. International capital flows have dried up and weak growth prospects resulted in a loss of market confidence and sharply rising interest rates, despite the fact that Portugal has steadfastly implemented an ambitious three year European Union-International Monetary Fund (EU-IMF) financial assistance programme since May 2011 (Box 1).

> ### Box 1. **The EU-IMF Adjustment Programme**
>
> In May 2011, Portugal agreed with the European Union and the International Monetary Fund on a far-reaching reform programme to restore market confidence and raise potential growth. The three-year programme is backed by substantial international financing (around EUR 78 billion). The three main goals of the programme are: *i)* implementing a credible fiscal consolidation supported by structural fiscal measures and better fiscal control over public-private partnerships (PPPs) and state-owned enterprises (SOEs); *ii)* safeguarding the financial sector against disorderly deleveraging through market-based mechanisms supported by backed-up facilities; and *iii)* implementing deep structural reforms to boost potential growth, create jobs, and improve competitiveness (including through fiscal devaluation). Quarterly reports published by the EU and the IMF indicate satisfactory programme implementation, with quantitative performance criteria met, as well as most structural benchmarks, albeit some with minor delays. This box presents the main measures already implemented or in the course of implementation.
>
> Regarding **public finance management**, the government is implementing a new Budgetary Framework Law, which includes multi-annual budgeting; a Fiscal Council was created and is progressively becoming operational; a new Commitments Law aims to ensure better control of expenditures and to tackle payment arrears; the first stage of the merger of tax and customs administrations was executed; a fiscal adjustment programme for the Madeira Autonomous Region was launched; a support program for local administration was agreed upon; quarterly budget reporting for the general government is in place; new local and regional financing laws are to be presented by the end of 2012; and costs are being reduced in SOEs, with the aim to reach operational balance for most of them in 2012.
>
> Concerning the **financial sector**, a special onsite inspection program has reviewed the banks' loan portfolio; most banks have already been recapitalised through private and public funds to meet both European Banking Authority (EBA) and Bank of Portugal Core Tier 1 targets; the bank resolution framework is being redesigned; and bank deleveraging is being carefully monitored.
>
> On the **labour market**, the authorities approved a new labour code, agreed with social partners, including one of the main confederations of unions; the changes include a reduction in severance payments, more flexible individual dismissals and working time arrangements, reduction of overtime pay, and some more scope for firm-level wage negotiations. Further reduction of severance entitlements is expected as well as the creation of out of court procedures to settle labour disputes.

> **Box 1. The EU-IMF Adjustment Programme** *(cont.)*
>
> To enhance the **business environment**, the government amended the insolvency regime to support the early rescue of viable firms; the transposition of the Professional Qualifications Directive is underway; a "zero authorisation" project to minimise licensing costs is being introduced, although difficulties remain in making it fully operational; the reform of the judicial system is reallocating judicial resources (new judicial map) and a new code of civil procedure will be submitted by end 2012 to speed up the judicial process; a new urban lease law was approved, aiming at faster eviction procedures and introducing a sunset clause of five years for most old contracts under rent control; a new Competition Law has been approved, increasing the responsibilities of the Competition Authority, and new competition and intellectual property courts have been created; a new arbitration law has been adopted; and a review of the main national regulators is underway. Privatisations of energy companies EDP and REN with significant premiums over market prices have yielded EUR 3.3 billon, or two-thirds of expected privatisation receipts under the programme.
>
> To **reduce rents in sheltered sectors** of the economy, the authorities are engaged in a number of renegotiation processes. In electricity, the review of contracts and subsidies to producers will lower the expected cumulative real price growth until 2020 by about one-sixth, while in the telecom sector, mobile termination rates will decrease considerably; measures aim to reduce the public cost of pharmaceuticals from 1.5% of gross domestic product (GDP) to 1% of GDP in 2013; a full review of all 36 PPPs by an international auditor has been completed with a view of possible contract renegotiations.

The programme is expected to remain on track but the balance of risks to growth is skewed to the downside. The size of the consolidation in 2012 is very large and the risk that fiscal targets are not met because growth undershoots expectations in a credit constrained and weak international environment is significant. Therefore, the government faces additional challenges to regain full market access within the programme period.

Against this uncertain backdrop, this Economic Survey examines progress in implementing structural reforms required to boost growth and reduce imbalances, while achieving fiscal consolidation (Annex A1). Chapter 1 discusses structural fiscal reforms and the pace of fiscal consolidation. This is followed by an analysis of the reforms to rebalance the economy, such as how to reinforce financial stability, improve labour market performance and achieve better investment allocation (Chapter 2).

The most pressing policy challenge is to stabilise the economy

The economy has started rebalancing, but the situation remains fragile. The huge current account deficit has dropped to 6.4% of gross domestic product (GDP) in 2011 (from 10% in 2010), due to weak domestic demand and strong exports that have resulted in sizeable gains in market share (Figure 1). Strong export performance reflects robust growth across a wide range of exported goods and services, most prominently in transport equipment, and has been accompanied by increased geographic diversification. Limited prospects at home are arguably pushing firms to become more export oriented and they have been helped by recent improvements in cost competitiveness (Figure 1), which go beyond the impact of cuts in public wages. Ensuring a sustainable correction of external imbalances – i.e. lasting beyond the short run internal demand contraction – will require further cost and non-cost competitiveness gains through labour cost restraint and productivity growth, supported by wide-ranging structural reforms.

Figure 1. **Key indicators**

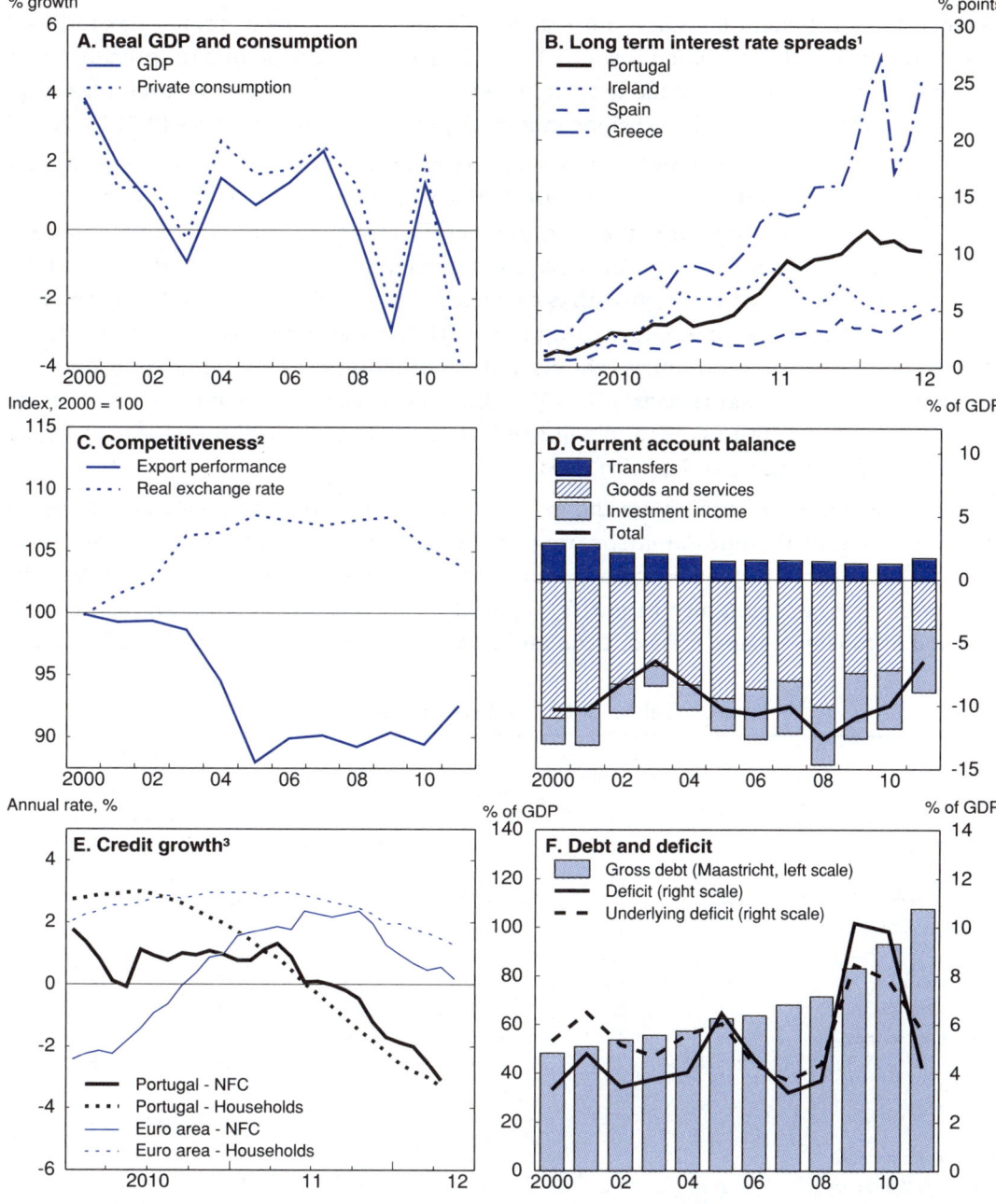

1. Ten-year government bond spreads relative to the German rate.
2. Export performance is the ratio between export volumes and export markets for total goods and services. The real exchange rate is a harmonised competitiveness indicator based on unit labour cost indices for the total economy.
3. Loans adjusted for sales and securitisation. NFC: non-financial corporations. Households includes non-profit institutions serving households.

Source: OECD (2012), *OECD Economic Outlook: Statistics and Projections* and *Main Economic Indicators* (databases), July; ECB (2012), *Statistical Data Warehouse*, European Central Bank, July; and Bank of Portugal (2012), *Indicadores de Conjuntura*, June.

StatLink ⟶ http://dx.doi.org/10.1787/888932669382

ASSESSMENT AND RECOMMENDATIONS

Since 2010, fiscal consolidation has gathered pace, weighing on public consumption and investment, and on household disposable income (Figure 1). Despite large-scale reliance on Eurosystem liquidity and resilient deposits, bank deleveraging has induced credit strains, which intensified towards the end of 2011, also weighing on private sector demand. Private consumption alone is expected to shrink by about 13% in 2011-13, a large fall even by the standards of recessions induced by excessive indebtedness (IMF, 2012).

Tight credit conditions and a worsening external environment are deepening the recession in 2012 (Table 1). As the result of fiscal improvement in 2011 being partly attributable to sizeable one-offs, the plan to meet fiscal targets in 2012 is very ambitious and will depress demand further. As global conditions improve, exports accelerate and the pace of fiscal contraction eases, growth is projected to gradually pick up in the second half of 2013. However, rising unemployment, along with the waning impact of indirect taxes hikes and of the rise in oil prices, should reduce inflation over the projection horizon. Following the substantial reduction in 2011, the current account deficit will continue to shrink. The public debt-to-GDP ratio will rise further in 2013, but will then begin to fall as the fiscal deficit narrows and growth rises.

Downside risks are mainly on the external side. Increasing turbulence caused by an intensification of the euro area sovereign debt crisis could undermine confidence in Portugal's prospects, penalising exports and further increasing credit strains. Domestically, the credit squeeze could also intensify, especially if necessary bank deleveraging were pursued at too fast a pace. Indeed, a too rapid and simultaneous deleveraging of both the

Table 1. **Short-term outlook**

	Current prices (billion euros) 2008	Percentage change, volume 2006 prices[1]				
		2009	2010	2011	2012	2013
Real gross domestic product	172.0	-2.9	1.4	-1.5	-3.2	-0.9
Private consumption	115.0	-2.3	2.1	-3.9	-6.8	-3.2
Government consumption	34.5	4.7	0.9	-3.9	-2.9	-2.4
Gross fixed capital formation	38.6	-8.6	-4.1	-11.4	-10.1	-3.2
Stockbuilding[2]	1.2	-1.1	0.1	-0.4	0.4	0.0
Total domestic demand	189.3	-3.2	0.8	-5.7	-6.4	-3.0
Exports of goods and services	55.8	-10.9	8.8	7.4	3.4	5.1
Imports of goods and services	73.1	-10.0	5.4	-5.5	-5.7	-0.1
Net exports[2]	-17.3	0.7	0.6	4.4	3.5	2.1
Memorandum items						
GDP deflator	..	0.9	1.1	0.6	0.1	0.4
Consumer price index (harmonised)	..	-0.9	1.4	3.6	3.1	0.7
Unemployment rate (% of labour force)	..	9.5	10.8	12.8	15.4	16.2
Household saving ratio[3]	..	10.9	10.2	9.7	10.5	12.1
General government financial balance[4]	..	-10.2	-9.8	-4.2	-4.6	-3.5
General government financial balance (net of one offs)[4]	..	-9.8	-8.8	-7.3	-5.4	-4.3
Gross government debt (Maastricht definition)[4]	..	83.1	93.3	107.8	114.5	120.3
Current account balance[4]	..	-10.9	-10.0	-6.4	-4.0	-2.2

1. Projections from 2012 onwards. The cut-off date for these projections was 15 May 2012.
2. Contribution to changes in real GDP (percentage of real GDP in previous year), actual amount in the first column.
3. Gross, as a percentage of disposable income.
4. As a percentage of GDP. Debt figures include the following cumulative amounts for Bank Solvency Support Facility: EUR 1 billion in 2011 (0.6% of GDP), EUR 8 billion in 2012 (4.8% of GDP) and EUR 12 billion in 2013 (7.2% of GDP).

Source: OECD (2012), *OECD Economic Outlook: Statistics and Projections* (database), May.

private and public sector entails the risk of fuelling recession. On the upside, exports have performed well recently and could continue to grow above expectations. Successful implementation of the programme could also boost confidence and domestic demand.

Raising growth in a sustainable way is the long-run challenge

Stronger long-run economic growth is required to raise living standards and enable Portugal to durably reduce its high levels of public and external debt. Over the past decade, potential growth has been hampered by a declining contribution from both employment and productivity (Figure 2), which underscores the need to improve on both counts. Employment has ceased to contribute to growth altogether, whereas trend productivity convergence to much higher euro area levels has slowed down substantially. Despite recent progress in export performance and market diversification, international trade is low given the small size of Portugal's economy; the average of exports and imports over GDP was only 37% in 2011, versus 43% for the average EU country. Moreover, investment has been to a large extent directed towards non-tradable sectors, often with little benefit for productivity growth.

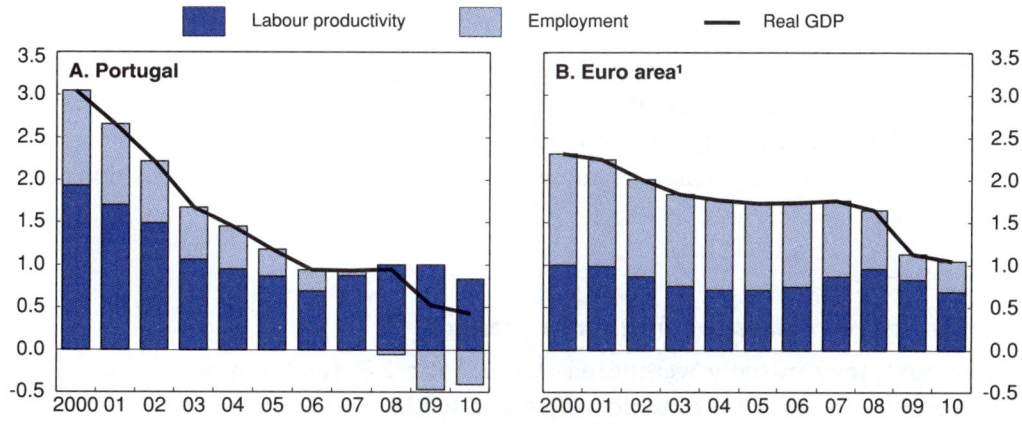

Figure 2. **Potential growth**
Contribution of employment and labour productivity to potential GDP growth, per cent

1. Euro area countries that are also OECD countries.
Source: OECD (2012), *OECD Economic Outlook: Statistics and Projections* (database), May.
StatLink ⟶ http://dx.doi.org/10.1787/888932669401

Weak productivity and trade need to be further tackled by reducing government-directed investment in transport infrastructure, incentives to homeownership and economic rents in general, so as to facilitate resource reallocation towards the tradable sector. A more flexible and less dualistic labour market would yield productivity gains through better job matching, improved incentives to invest in human capital and also enhanced competition between firms. Product market reforms in sheltered sectors would enhance productivity growth by spurring innovation. Combined labour and product markets reforms would make the economy more attractive for export-oriented foreign direct investment (FDI) and have the potential to yield employment gains relatively fast (OECD, 2012). Ambitious reforms currently being implemented by the authorities in these directions and further steps needed are discussed below.

Raising growth and living standards sustainably will also require continuing efforts to contribute to climate change mitigation and – more generally – to make a more efficient use of environmental resources in consumption and production. Portugal's energy-related carbon dioxide (CO_2) emissions are low in international comparison, both in per capita and in relation to GDP, as are greenhouse gas emissions, and the country has made further progress over the past 10 years. Environmentally-friendly policies, in addition to sectoral change, have contributed to these improvements.

The government has placed a strong emphasis on increasing the share of renewable energy generation, the share of environmentally related revenues is higher than the OECD average and the share of public research and development (R&D) spending related to the environment is among the highest in the OECD (OECD, 2011a).

Portugal has made good progress in reducing air pollutants, with sulphur oxide emissions declining by more than 60% – well above the average in the OECD – and nitrogen oxide emissions by more than 10%. However, the level of nitrogen emissions is high in relation to GDP compared to other countries. Around 40% of these emissions are due to road transport. Local air pollution incidents related to ground level ozone concentrations still occur in large cities and combined with high levels of particulate matter from the growing number of diesel vehicles, pose threats to human health. Portugal should encourage greater use of existing public transport infrastructure including through better road pricing to tackle these issues.

Agricultural pollution is also of concern due to a highly intensive use of pesticides and fishing enterprises exploit some species beyond biologically safe limits (OECD, 2011b). As discussed below, given the tight fiscal position, achieving environmental goals will more than ever necessitate using policy instruments that benefit both the fiscal position and the environment.

Financial stability

The crisis has put domestic banks under pressure

Although they initially weathered the global crisis relatively well, thanks to no substantial direct exposure to toxic assets and to the absence of a real estate bubble, Portuguese banks have been particularly vulnerable to a shift in investor sentiment owing to excessive reliance on foreign borrowing and a major increase in exposure to government bonds (especially in 2010). The sovereign debt crisis led to a loss of access to wholesale debt markets in 2010, forcing banks into reliance on Eurosystem financing. Banking system net income turned negative in 2011, largely due to growing credit impairments and the materialisation of market risks, such as losses in financial assets portfolios, but also due to several non-recurring events.

Bank deleveraging is tightening credit

To reinforce financial stability and ease the return to wholesale market funding, banks are raising Core Tier 1 ratios to comply with targets set by Bank of Portugal (10% at end-2012) and, for four of the largest groups, by the European Banking Authority (9% by 30 June 2012, computed under slightly different and more demanding rules, plus a capital buffer for sovereign exposures). For this purpose, some private banks will need public funds, which will be provided under the EUR 12 billion Bank Solvency Support Facility (BSSF) included in the financial envelope of the EU-IMF programme. In June, the government provided public funds to three major banks, allowing them to comply with both of those requirements in terms of solvency ratios. To increase reliance on more stable sources of funding, the eight largest banking groups (accounting for 83% of the banking system's assets) are also reducing their individual loan-to-deposit ratios to an indicative target of about 120%, to be met by end-2014. Mostly due to a surge in deposits (Figure 3), fuelled by shifts in the composition of households' financial asset portfolios, notably as a reaction to bank financial incentives (higher rates on deposit accounts), the eight banks as a whole have lowered their ratio to about 130% at end-2011, a 30 percentage points reduction from June 2010. However, further deposit growth will likely be more moderate, and there is considerable dispersion across banks in loan-to-deposit ratios. While five banks are already below, or very close to, the indicative 120% target, the other three major banks were still above 140% at the end of 2011.

Bank deleveraging is increasingly taking place via credit contraction (Figure 1). Constraints to credit supply, especially for firms, may be aggravating recessionary dynamics in the economy. The Euro Area Bank Lending Survey points to a considerable tightening of loans to firms, which is more intense than the contraction in firms' credit demand. Sectoral surveys also show credit constraints, which are highest in construction, but have been increasing also in manufacturing and services. Small and medium-sized enterprises (SME) have been on the whole more affected than large firms, some of which have access to external financing. The strong rise until recently in interest rates for new loans (Figure 3) partly reflects higher rates on deposits, although pressure on deposit rates has been eased by participation by Portuguese banks in the recent three-year European Central Bank (ECB) long-term refinancing operations and additional capital requirements for deposits paying high rates (introduced in November 2011 by the Bank of Portugal to tame excessive bank competition for deposits). Spreads between new loans and new deposit rates, which are becoming higher in international comparison (Figure 3), reflect the rise in the overall credit risk and uncertainty in the Portuguese economy.

While higher capital ratios and lower loan-to-deposit ratios are essential for financial stability, bank deleveraging risks aggravating credit contraction, as mentioned previously. The authorities should ensure that the pace of convergence towards the indicative loan-to-deposit ratio target of about 120% by end-2014 does not thwart economic activity. This degree of flexibility is made more important by the fact that those banks further away from the target have on average a larger weight of loans to firms in their portfolios. More generally, to minimise the risk of credit rationing, the authorities should keep the remainder of the EUR 12 billion envelope for further capital increases if needed, even after 2012 capital targets are met, as losses from credit impairments put downward pressure on risk-weighted assets. In bank recapitalisation operations, the authorities should pay attention that the potential costs to taxpayers and the final beneficiaries of the funds are fully transparent so as to reduce moral hazard and maintain public support (IMF, 2009).

Reducing barriers to efficient credit allocation

Removing distortions to credit reallocation across sectors would foster productivity-enhancing shifts in investment composition. Over the past decade, credit has been overwhelmingly directed towards construction-related activities and other sheltered sectors, to the detriment of tradables (Figure 4). Recent developments do not yet indicate a significant reversal of those trends. While loans to construction and real estate have

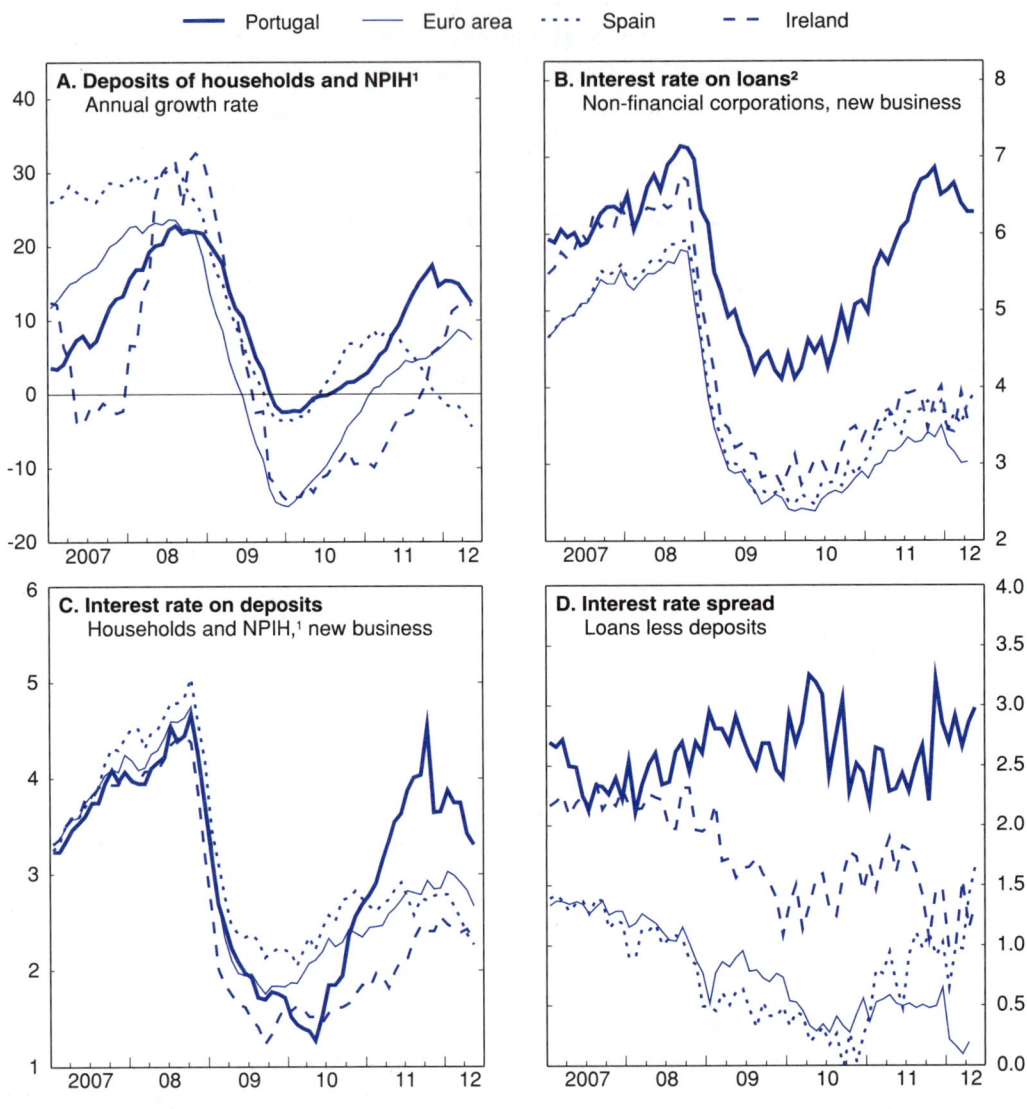

Figure 3. **Banking sector indicators**
Per cent

1. NPIH: non-profit institutions serving households.
2. Loans other than revolving loans and overdrafts, convenience and extended credit card debt.
Source: ECB (2012), "Money, Banking and Financial Markets", Statistical Data Warehouse, European Central Bank, July.
StatLink ⟶ http://dx.doi.org/10.1787/888932669420

started to shrink markedly, credit to the transportation, education and healthcare sectors has continued to expand. State-owned enterprises (SOE) are important players in these sectors, although they only account for about 5% of outstanding credit to non-financial corporations, as a large part of them has been reclassified within the general government sector.

On-going efforts to improve SOE operational performance will gradually ease financing pressures, while a number of measures foreseen in the 2012 Supplementary Budget will more immediately ease credit reallocation and help defuse credit strains. These include up to EUR 3 billion of credit assignment from the banks to the central government for loans to local governments, hospitals and SOEs inside general government, while maintaining the obligations of the debtors. In addition, measures will include a

Figure 4. **Loans of financial institutions to households and non-financial corporations**[1]

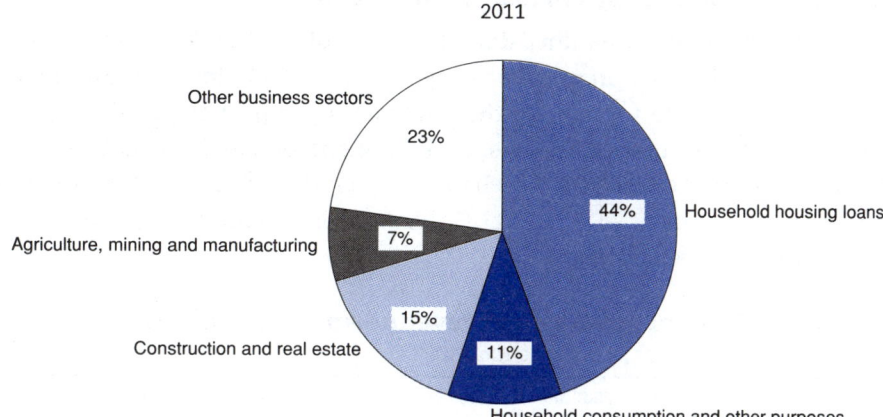

1. Financial institutions excluding the Central Bank. Total loans of EUR 257 billion, average of end of month figures.
Source: Bank of Portugal (2012), *Boletim Estatístico*, June.

StatLink ᔥ http://dx.doi.org/10.1787/888932669439

EUR 1.5 billion settlement of arrears by the state to public hospitals outside general government and EUR 1 billion to repay local government arrears. More generally, credit reallocation will be fostered by removing distortions which have favoured investment in sheltered sectors, such as housing, transport infrastructure or energy, as addressed elsewhere in this Survey.

It is also essential that banks refrain from "ever-greening" problematic loans, and continue to clean up their balance sheets. International experience, not least from Japan in the 1990s, shows that delaying loss recognition tends to depress productivity growth, slow economic recovery and thus increase total costs to be borne either by the private or the public sector (OECD, 2012). Non-performing loans reached 7.5% of total loans in December 2011, with the steepest rises in construction and real estate. The central bank's supervisory capabilities have been strengthened following the Special Inspections Programme, which examined the credit portfolios and stress-testing methods of the eight largest banking groups (with overall positive results), and banks have been required to identify all instances of restructured loans (even if still performing) due to financial difficulties of the borrower. The authorities should continue to use supervisory tools to promote swift recognition of bad loans.

Box 2. Core recommendations on financial stability

- Remove barriers to credit reallocation by tackling incentives to investment in sheltered sectors and "ever-greening" of problematic loans.
- In bank recapitalisation operations, ensure that the potential costs to taxpayers and the final beneficiaries of the funds are fully transparent.
- Pay special attention to financing conditions of small and medium-sized enterprises, notably by making firms more reliant on equity and by re-directing EU funds.
- Ensure that the pace of convergence towards the indicative target for the loan-to-deposit ratio does not thwart economic activity.

Fiscal policy

Significant risks remain on the path to debt sustainability

The government achieved a headline deficit of 4.2% of GDP in 2011, less than half the 2010 deficit and lower than the programme target (5.9% of GDP). However, this included significant one-offs, notably the transfer to the government of private pension assets of 3.5% of GDP – in exchange for future liabilities. Excluding one-offs and cyclical effects, the underlying deficit was around 6% of GDP, which implies that the actual fiscal consolidation in 2011 was only about 2 points of GDP in 2011 (Table 2). This is nonetheless a remarkable achievement compared to previous years.

Table 2. **General government revenue and expenditure**
Per cent of GDP

	1995-2000	2001-08	2009	2010	2011	2012[1]	2013[1]
Current revenue	36.4	38.9	38.8	38.7	40.3	40.5	40.9
Current expenditure	38.2	42.5	47.9	47.8	47.4	46.5	46.2
Gross saving	–1.8	–3.6	–9.1	–9.1	–7.2	–6.0	–5.3
Total revenue	37.7	40.4	39.6	41.4	44.7	42.0	42.7
Total expenditure	41.7	44.7	49.8	51.3	48.9	46.6	46.2
Net lending	–4.0	–4.3	–10.2	–9.8	–4.2	–4.6	–3.5
Memorandum items							
Underlying fiscal balance[2]	–4.8	–5.1	–8.5	–7.9	–5.8	–2.4	–0.8
Underlying primary balance[2]	–1.4	–2.6	–5.9	–5.1	–2.3	1.4	2.9
Gross debt (Maastricht definition)	53.3	60.5	83.1	93.3	107.8	114.5	120.3
Net debt	30.3	45.9	64.5	63.7	54.0	81.2	85.1
Capital transfers and payments	0.8	0.7	1.0	2.0	1.2	0.6	0.8
Capital tax and transfers receipts	1.2	1.5	0.7	2.7	4.4	1.5	1.8

1. Projections.
2. Per cent of potential GDP. The underlying balances are adjusted for the cycle and for one-offs. For more details, see *OECD Economic Outlook* Sources and Methods.
Source: OECD (2012), OECD Economic Outlook: Statistics and Projections (database), May.

The government targets a headline fiscal deficit of 4½ per cent of GDP in 2012 and 3% in 2013 as part of the EU-IMF programme (Table 3). Due to the need to make up for the large one-offs in 2011, such targets will require a large underlying fiscal consolidation of about 3½ per cent of GDP in 2012 – 1½ percentage point more than in 2011 – and about 1½ per cent of GDP in 2013. To achieve this, the government is using a wide range of measures in 2012, of which around two thirds are on the expenditure side and one third on the revenue side. They include reducing wages and staff in the public service, cutting pensions, increasing the list of goods and services taxed at the standard value-added tax (VAT) rate and reducing tax expenditures. The government expects public debt to peak at 116% of GDP by 2013 before declining.

The expected pace of consolidation between 2011 and 2013 is among the most rapid in the OECD (Figure 5). On the one hand, major consolidation is needed to restore debt sustainability and convince markets that Portugal can exit from the programme and return to the bond market within the programme horizon. On the other hand, fiscal consolidation reduces growth which could, in turn, undermine political support and market confidence.

Addressing this trade-off regarding the speed of consolidation is made more difficult by large macroeconomic uncertainties. In an attempt to take these uncertainties into account, the OECD has carried out simulations using a small stylised macroeconomic model where

Table 3. **Stability Programme targets and assumptions**
Per cent of GDP[1]

	2010	2011	Targets and assumptions				
			2012	2013	2014	2015	2016
Public balance	−9.8	−4.2	−4.5	−3.0	−1.8	−1.0	−0.5
Expenditure	51.3	48.9	47.5	45.9	44.6	43.8	43.0
Revenue	41.4	44.7	42.9	42.9	42.8	42.7	42.5
Public debt (Maastricht definition)	93.3	107.8	113.1	115.7	113.4	109.5	103.9
Real GDP growth (%)	1.4	−1.5	−3.0	0.6	2.0	2.4	2.8

1. Revenue and balance include a number of one-offs of which the most notable is a positive one in 2011 of 3½ per cent of GDP corresponding to the transfer to the government of the assets of banks' pension funds, in exchange for overtaking future pension liabilities.
Source: OECD (2012), OECD Economic Outlook: Statistics and Projections (database), May for historical series of 2010-11 and Ministry of Finance (2012), Documento de Estratégia Orçamental 2012-16 for targets and assumptions of 2012-16.

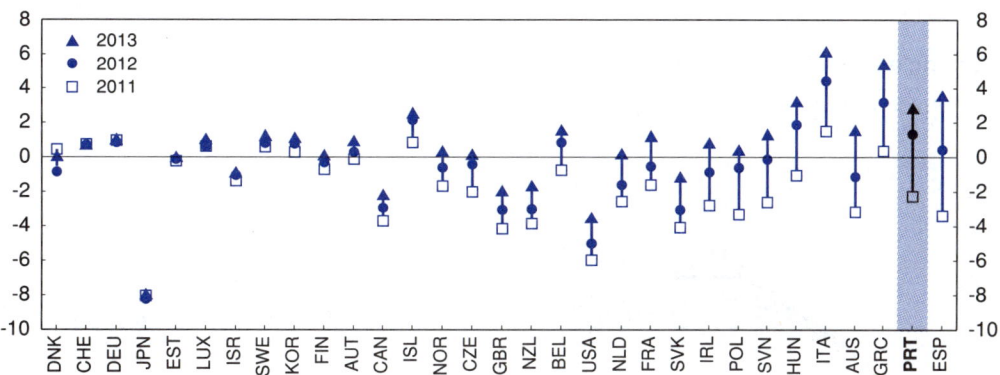

Figure 5. **Fiscal consolidation in international comparison**
Underlying government primary balance, per cent of potential GDP[1]

1. Countries are sorted in order of total fiscal consolidation between 2011 and 2013.
Source: OECD (2012), OECD Economic Outlook: Statistics and Projections (database), May.

StatLink http://dx.doi.org/10.1787/888932669458

variables are affected by random shocks (Sorbe, 2012; Figure 6). The results suggest that sticking to the programme's nominal deficit targets would almost certainly put debt on a declining path over the medium term, but with a significant risk of a deeper recession and higher unemployment. In contrast, letting automatic stabilisers play would limit the recession risk, but at a significant risk that the debt-to-GDP ratio will continue to rise. On balance and given the need to restore confidence, the government should aim at meeting its nominal fiscal targets as long as growth does not deviate substantially from the programme. Nevertheless, should downside risks materialise and output fall substantially more than projected in the programme, the automatic stabilisers could be allowed to play, at least partially.

These debt simulations also show that risks around the fiscal consolidation programme would be minimised by stimulating potential growth through structural reforms and by choosing "growth friendly" fiscal consolidation instruments. In addition, an appropriate choice of consolidation instruments could lower the size of the fiscal multipliers, reducing the risks of aggravated recession when sticking to nominal deficit targets. The choice of consolidation instruments should also take into account the need to spread fairly the burden of adjustment across the population to maintain social consensus around the programme as well as, when relevant, environmental considerations.

Figure 6. **Assessing the risks around the fiscal consolidation programme**
Stochastic simulation results under different fiscal policy programmes[1]

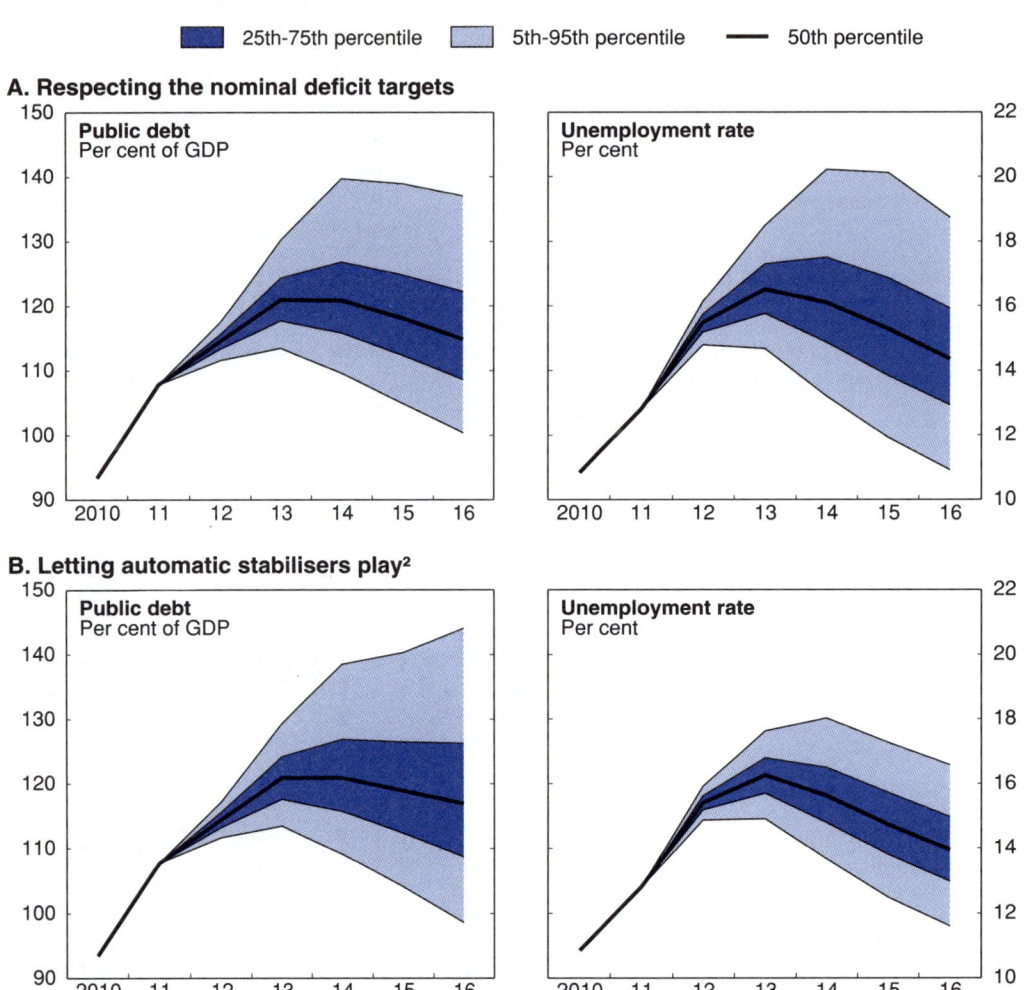

1. The likelihood of different debt and unemployment paths are shown with their attached probabilities, which are derived via Monte Carlo simulations on a small-scale stylised macroeconomic model where random shocks affect the different variables. The model notably takes into account the effect of financial conditions and of fiscal policy on activity, with a multiplier of 1. Interest rates on Portuguese bonds depend on a random parameter reflecting market confidence and on the debt dynamics in a non-linear way, allowing rates to explode if debt is seen as out of control. The baseline scenario is based on OECD projections (*OECD Economic Outlook* No. 91) until 2013, prolonged from 2014 onwards with the assumptions from IMF (2012), "Portugal: Third Review Under the Extended Agreement" and the targets presented in Table 3 for public deficit.
2. Respecting the structural primary deficit targets.
Source: S. Sorbe (2012), "Portugal: Assessing the Risks about the Speed of Fiscal Consolidation in an Uncertain Environment", *OECD Economics Department Working Papers*, forthcoming.

StatLink http://dx.doi.org/10.1787/888932669477

There are strong pressures on the government's cash position

The sovereign debt crisis has created financing problems across the general government, as SOEs inside general government as well as local and regional governments no longer have access to market finance to cover deficits and payment arrears or to roll over existing debts. The central government is able to borrow using short-term treasury bills and has been doing so – with longer maturities and declining yields over the last few months – *inter alia* to meet SOE and local government needs (for example to repay SOE debt owed to banks). However, the risk that less financing is available from this source still exists. The government is currently proposing to meet hospital payment arrears using pension funds transferred from the banking sector. This transfer needs to be transparent and accompanied by strong incentives for hospitals to prevent further accumulation of arrears. There is a substantial risk in the current recessionary and credit-constrained environment that more SOEs currently outside the general government could fall into financing difficulties, putting further pressure on the government's already stretched resources and risking reclassification into general government, further increasing the fiscal deficit and debt.

Improving expenditure control and transparency

Since entry to the euro was confirmed in 1998, the government, with the exception of a brief period at the peak of the global boom in the mid-2000s, persistently raised spending as a fraction of GDP (Figure 7). This came mainly from over-optimistic economic and revenue forecasts, and therefore expenditure plans, which is a common failing internationally (Hagemann, 2010). In addition, the authorities failed to meet those plans. Budget enforcement has also been impeded by fragmented, infrequent and limited financial reporting with financially autonomous units of the government not being held sufficiently accountable for over-spending.

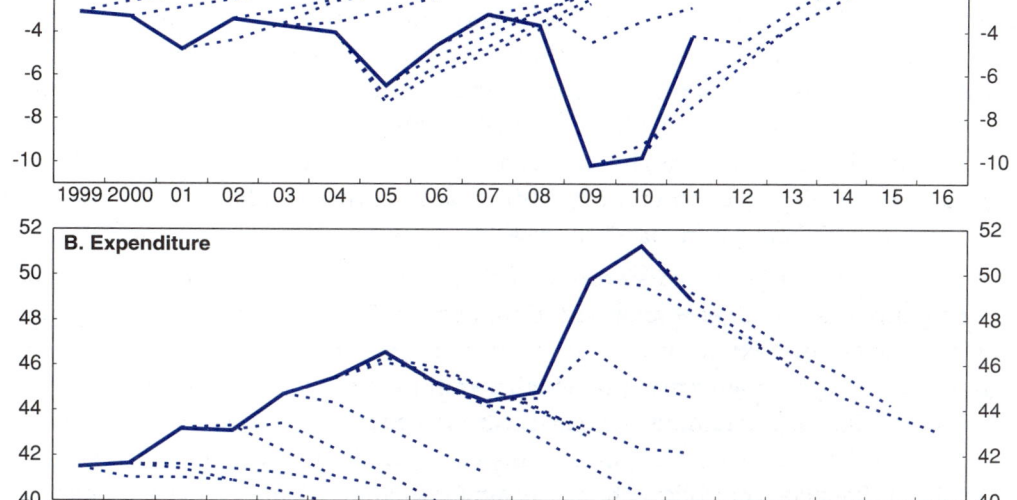

Figure 7. **Forecasts for general government net lending and expenditure**
Based on Stability and Growth Programmes, per cent of GDP[1]

1. To take account of periodic revisions to GDP, projected programme target paths for the net lending and expenditure to GDP ratios have been appended to initial starting levels rebased to the most recent data vintage for these series.
Source: Ministry of Finance (2011 and 2012), *Documento de Estratégia Orçamental*; Portuguese Republic (1998-2010), *Stability and Growth Programmes* and OECD (2012), *OECD Economic Outlook: Statistics and Projections* (database), May.
StatLink http://dx.doi.org/10.1787/888932669496

Budget control has been further hampered by the non-transparent build-up of substantial liabilities to provide subsidised health and transport services. This has been partly achieved by shifting the spending burden of policy decisions into the future through the heavy use of public-private partnerships (PPP). In addition, private sector (telecom and banking) pension assets were transferred to the government in 2010 and 2011 with a positive impact in general government accounts in these years, but increasing public expenditure in the future. This type of one-off should be avoided as it ultimately undermines the fiscal position and reduces fiscal credibility. In addition, SOEs have run substantial losses, which in the case of hospitals have been covered by accumulating large payments arrears. A similar strategy has been followed at the local level. Total wider government payment arrears, including SOEs not inside general government, totalled 3.2% of GDP in early 2012. Overall, this opacity surrounding the full general government position allowed the government to avoid taking corrective actions in the short-run but has ultimately exacerbated the fiscal crisis.

The enhanced fiscal framework is welcome

The enhanced medium-term fiscal framework introduced in May 2011 provides a strong stepping stone for tackling fiscal problems. Its main elements include: in line with European requirements, a medium-term structural deficit of no more than 0.5% of GDP; a rolling budget planning that sets expenditure ceilings for the central government for the next four years; an independent fiscal council; and programme budgeting. The expansion of the State Budget reporting perimeter to the national accounts definition of general government and the progressive implementation of monthly reporting for the whole of general government are also welcome.

The framework could be better anchored and made more transparent by adding an expenditure rule for general government consistent with revenue projections and the deficit target and in line with the European fiscal framework. Such a rule would help to prevent the upward creep in spending that has characterised policy until recently and ensure that all general government spending is under control. Compliance is easily observed (unlike a structural deficit), and it would not be especially procyclical in that most automatic stabilisers work through the revenue side. Given the need to reduce both the deficit and the scale of government spending, such a rule would initially have to set expenditure growth below nominal GDP growth.

Ensuring that the framework truly contributes to fiscal sustainability will require improving important budget implementation, notably fully enacting the new system of stricter intra-annual expenditure control measures. Centred on 14 main spending programmes, this system aims to restrain both commitments and cash outlays. However, the technical capability of programme financial controllers to carry out these oversight functions and interact with the Ministry of Finance varies across ministries. To instil a greater sense of responsibility, financial controllers should be appointments assigned to named individuals rather than simply a function assigned to the head of the planning unit for example. In addition they should have sufficient time to properly carry out these functions and have access to analytical support staff, which is currently not the case in all ministries.

The Fiscal Council has an important role to play in assessing the government's compliance with the new framework. The resources available to it should be commensurate with its wide remit. To remove a serious constraint on recruitment, the government should relax the prohibition on board members and staff having other paid, or any other employment at all, respectively. In the first instance the Council should prioritise core functions, including assessing the macroeconomic and fiscal projections and compliance with fiscal rules as well as giving fiscal policy recommendations. There is evidence that fiscal councils that provide policy recommendations, rather than just analysis, are more effective (Debrun *et al.*, 2009). The Council's role should be further embedded in the policy debate by requiring the Minister of Finance to provide a formal response in Parliament to Fiscal Council reports.

Improve operational performance of SOEs

In 2011 the SOE sector lost EUR 1.9 billion (1.1% of GDP) on total assets of EUR 55.8 billion (32% of GDP). SOEs in the urban passenger transport, rail and hospital sub-sectors have been making large losses (Figure 8). These losses are due to large debt-servicing burdens as well as operational losses. The government aims to stop these operational losses and achieve operational balance in all SOEs excluding the rail track company and the health sector by the end of 2012 and data for the first quarter of 2012 point to an improvement of the situation. An examination of the accounts of the worst loss-making companies in the public transport sector suggests that better controlling labour and supplier costs will be important. It may also be necessary to continue rationalising the regional rail network as most operational losses occurred in providing these services.

Figure 8. **State-owned enterprise performance**
By industry/company, in million euros at end 2011[1]

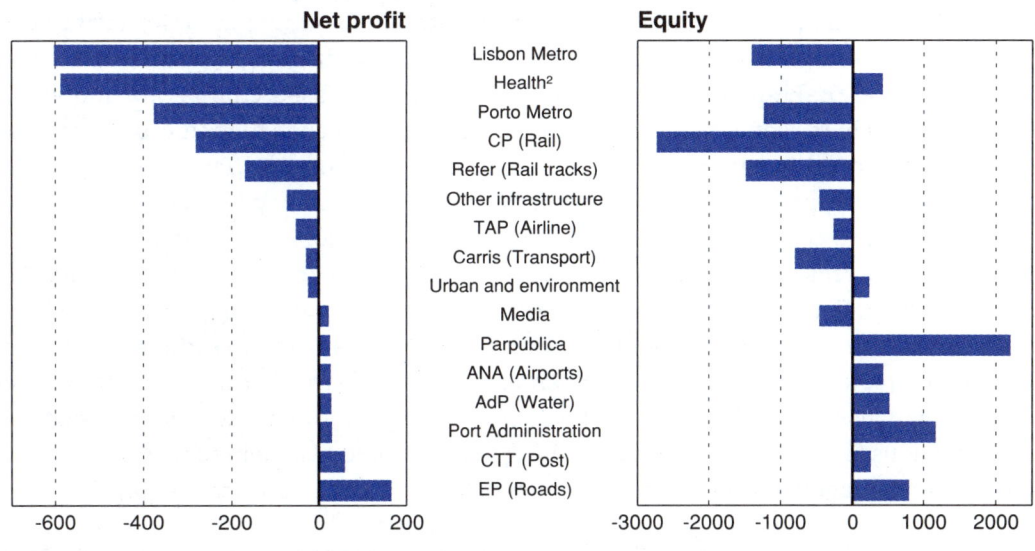

1. 2010 for TAP.
2. Losses in the health sector include those of a new hospital whose revenue was not fully recorded in 2011.
Source: Ministry of Finance (2012), *Boletim Informativo Sobre o Sector Empresarial do Estado: 4.º Trimestre 2011* and Parpública (2011), *Documentos de Prestação de Contas 2010*.

StatLink ⟶ http://dx.doi.org/10.1787/888932669515

PPP decision making should be incorporated into the medium-term budget framework

Portugal engaged in the highest value of PPP contracts relative to GDP in Europe in the period 1990-2010, mainly for building highways (Kappeler and Nemoz, 2010; EPEC, 2010). The flow of future net government payments associated with these projects is expected to increase to almost 1% of GDP in 2015 as the latest wave of roads comes on line. The immediate policy challenge is to limit the costs and risks associated with these existing projects. To reduce costs, a mixture of measures could be taken, depending on the exact circumstances of each PPP, including: renegotiating terms; cancelling projects, when still at an early stage; or buying back the PPP (Reis, 2012, argues that buybacks would be appropriate for many road projects).

PPPs remain a potentially useful investment model. However, they should be chosen only when they represent good value for money, not because they allow the government to escape budget restrictions by building up off-balance sheet liabilities. The policy framework for PPPs compares well internationally on paper but the government lacked technical expertise and political considerations interfered. It is therefore important that the decision making process for future PPPs take full account of the analysis of the new technical advisory unit being set up in the Ministry of Finance. To encourage this, the analyses of the unit, including a comparison with an ordinary public investment alternative, should be made fully available to the parliament and public. The government should also further reform how PPPs are included in budget planning. PPPs should be accounted for on the same basis as the alternative of an ordinary public investment.

Environmental measures can pay multiple dividends

The decision to institute user tolls on formerly free PPP highways is appropriate from an environmental and fiscal point of view. The government is also planning, in tandem with municipalities, to develop a package of measures to promote the use of public transport, including extending bus lanes, and increasing parking restrictions and the cost of individual transport. The authorities should be ambitious in this area, for example by widening the coverage of and increasing parking fees, introducing congestion charges in major cities and making greater use of road tolls, as increased charges for individual transport can help to reduce congestion and air pollution which is high in urban areas (air particulates exceed EU air quality standards in the Lisbon and Porto areas). These measures can also provide fiscal revenue and increase efficiency by making users pay closer attention to the social costs of individual road transport. The government should also consider increasing the enforcement of sanctions for breaches of environmental law in areas such as fishing where applied fines are low by EU standards (OECD, 2011b) and fully support the recent European Commission proposal to introduce individual transferable quotas, which has been proven as a very efficient instrument to protect the resource (Haraldsson and Carey, 2011). Reducing tax expenditures, such as removing fuel tax exemptions for the agricultural and fishing sector, would also help to increase revenue as well as encouraging the switch to more fuel efficient and less polluting equipment.

Enhancing spending efficiency will be key to successful consolidation of local finances

A number of local and regional governments have failed to cut expenditure sufficiently in response to persistent revenue declines since 2009, leading to debt accumulation. After losing access to long-term bank financing in the wake of the sovereign debt crisis, they have been relying on short-term debt and payment arrears, notably through local public companies. The central government is auditing these liabilities, of which the total extent is still uncertain, and stepping in to provide support. It will lend EUR 1.5 billion (0.9% of GDP) to the autonomous region of Madeira in exchange for fiscal consolidation and enhanced monitoring. It also agreed to set a EUR 1 billion (0.6% of GDP) credit line to help municipalities reduce their reliance on short-term debts and arrears. Such support is welcome as long as it alleviates liquidity problems of solvent local or regional authorities. However, it should be granted according to strict and transparent guidelines to ensure equal treatment of municipalities and include tight monitoring to ensure debt control is quickly regained, including by requiring municipalities to keep their funds in a dedicated account at the Treasury. If certain authorities are judged insolvent, the government should be ready to accept defaults in some instances to promote prudent future local policymaking.

In a context of durably lower revenues, successful consolidation of local finances requires enhancing local spending efficiency. The government intends to present measures before the end of 2012, including a reorganisation of local public companies, a 30% reduction in the number of parishes (the lowest tier of local government) and more inter-municipal cooperation. These measures are welcome, and would be usefully complemented by the generalisation of benchmarking and performance indicators to narrow the large efficiency disparities across local governments (Afonso and Fernandes, 2003). In addition, tighter monitoring of local revenue forecasts is needed to avoid over-optimism leading to overspending. Measures should also be taken to make local revenues less volatile, such as a shift away from taxing housing transactions towards increased recurrent taxation on immovable property, as planned.

Value for money should be paramount in spending EU funds

Making better use of EU structural and cohesion funds would help mitigate the effects of spending cuts. The full absorption of available funds (about 2% of GDP per year) remains a challenge. Portugal is actively shifting money away from cancelled or postponed infrastructure projects, such as the Lisbon-Madrid high speed train, towards other programmes, notably education related ones. As a number of selected infrastructure projects are dormant because of financing constraints, such a strategic shift should continue and focus as much as possible on the most pressing economic challenges, like supporting financing to credit-squeezed SMEs (*e.g.* through credit lines) and preventing high unemployment from becoming structural (*e.g.* through targeted training programmes). The reduced local co-financing of EU projects will also stimulate the absorption of funds. However, as it lowers the financial risks borne by local stakeholders, it reinforces the need to improve governance to secure careful project selection and adequate monitoring. In this area, there is evidence of political interference in the allocation of funds to municipalities (Veiga, 2010), pointing to a need for more transparency, evaluation and accountability in the selection of public projects.

Retaining highly skilled public sector staff is essential to government efficiency

The ability of the government to implement policies depends crucially on the skill of its civil servants. The urgent need to consolidate the fiscal position means that staff and wages are being substantially cut in tandem with increases in workload. Moreover, wages of high-skilled civil servants in the areas of law or economics were already significantly lower than in the private sector before the crisis whereas lower skilled workers are generally paid a premium relative to the private sector (Campos and Pereira, 2009). The government's current room for manoeuvre is currently extremely constrained but in the medium term the wage schedule should be steepened and more flexible individual contracts for specialists introduced. Steepening the wage schedule would bring government sector pay more in line with that in the private sector thereby helping the government to continue to attract and maintain highly qualified staff.

> **Box 3. Core recommendations to improve fiscal performance**
>
> - The government should aim to meet headline deficit targets in the programme, notably through abiding by the budgeted expenditure at all levels of general government. If risks materialise significantly and growth is far lower than projected in the programme, the automatic stabilisers could be allowed to operate at least partially.
> - Introduce an explicit and easily enforceable public expenditure rule consistent with revenue projections and medium-term fiscal objectives and in line with the new European fiscal framework.
> - Support to local and regional governments should be accompanied with improvements in the fiscal framework. Municipalities should notably be required to keep their funds in a dedicated account at the Treasury.

Education, labour and social policies

Education remains the key to long-term prosperity and social cohesion

Low education levels across the workforce explain a substantial proportion of Portugal's productivity gap (OECD, 2010a). Fewer educated workers impede the labour force's capacity to quickly learn and adapt to the fast changing global environment. In 2009, only 30% of the working age population (25-64) had attained upper secondary education compared with 73% in the OECD. From a low base in the 1970s there have been marked improvements down the generations but there is still a long way to go. Progress in education has been uneven. Upper secondary attainment is still considerably behind other countries, around 60% of the OECD average for 25-34 year-olds (48% as against 81% for the OECD), while significant progress has been made on tertiary and post-tertiary education. Nevertheless, previous education reforms are paying off with PISA (Programme for International Student Assessment) scores in reading, mathematics and science rising over time to approach OECD averages (OECD, 2010b) and resources have been rationalised with the closure of many small schools as recommended in previous *Economic Surveys*.

To tackle high drop-out rates the government raised the school leaving age from 15 to 18 in 2009 and under the *Novas Oportunidades* programme massively increased vocational education and training (VET) at the upper secondary school level. To enhance the results of this approach the government should ensure: the right input mix including sufficient physical resources for VET courses, which tend to be equipment and materials intensive; adequate career guidance for students to inform on course choice; and a close partnership with business to ensure that training is labour market relevant. Recent policy actions, including giving firms more influence over training choice and attempts to better target training, go in the right direction but it will be important to track the labour market outcomes of training participants and adjust programmes accordingly.

The government has progressively added to the education assessment and evaluation framework, including introducing a new teacher appraisal system in 2007 (revised in 2010). However, the approach to assessment and evaluation is not integrated and there are some important data gaps. The focus is at all levels on assessment, with insufficient use of data to indicate ways to improve learning outcomes, teacher development, school performance and the policy framework of the whole system (Pereira, 2010; Santiago et al., 2012). To remedy this will require *inter alia* greater focus on "progress": collecting information over time on individuals and cohorts; instituting a development appraisal to complement the current assessment appraisal for teachers; and shifting resources towards greater analysis of system-wide results (Santiago et al., 2012).

High income inequality in Portugal is linked to the dispersion of educational attainment (Figure 9), reflecting that higher wages are associated with increasing education levels, which is exacerbated further by the fact that there is a higher premium earned for better education in Portugal than elsewhere due to a relative scarcity of skills (OECD, 2010a). The relationship is two-way with family background having a particularly strong influence on the probability of dropping out of school and participating in tertiary education in Portugal and there is a longer than average tail of children who fail to reach even the basic PISA skill level (OECD, 2010b). This argues for a stronger focus in the assessment and evaluation framework on improving education opportunities and learning outcomes of children from more deprived socio-economic backgrounds, which is currently lacking (Santiago et al., 2012). This would help to break down the inter-generational cycle of poverty as well as eventually helping to tackle high levels of informality.

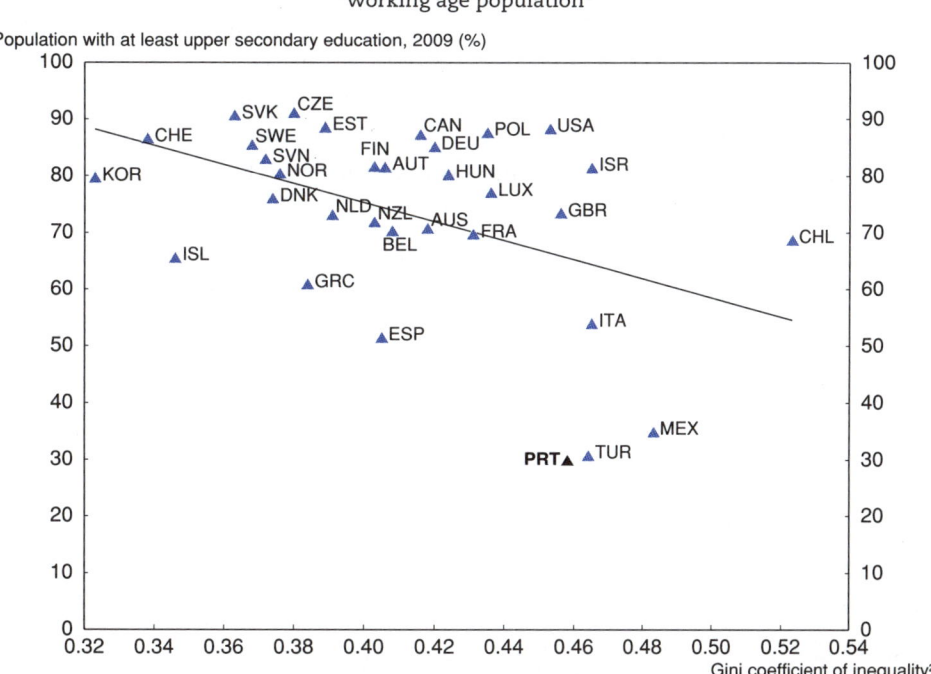

Figure 9. **Inequality and level of educational attainment**
Working age population[1]

1. Population aged 25-64 for upper secondary education and age 18-65 for the Gini coefficient.
2. Gini coefficient based on income before taxes and transfers. The values of the Gini coefficient range between 0, in the case of "perfect equality", and 1, in the case of "perfect inequality" (i.e. all income goes to the individual with the highest income). The data cover the latest year available which is 2008 or 2009 for most countries.
Source: OECD (2012), "Income Distribution: Inequality", OECD Social Expenditure Statistics (database), May and OECD (2011), Education at a Glance 2011.

StatLink ⟶ http://dx.doi.org/10.1787/888932669534

Maintaining social cohesion is an important pre-requisite for programme success

Maintaining social cohesion is an important challenge, especially against a background of high and rising unemployment. The government fostered social consensus through the tripartite agreement on labour reforms. Steps have also been taken to protect lower income individuals and place a greater share of the fiscal adjustment burden on higher income earners, for example by reducing tax credits and introducing an additional higher income tax rate for top earners. In addition, public sector pay cuts and income tax changes have led to greater percentage income falls for high income earners, having clauses to protect the lowest income brackets. However, consolidations tend to have adverse impacts on income distribution (Ahrend et al., 2011), and there is some indication that certain measures between 2009 and mid-2011 may have been regressive (Callan et al., 2011). In addition, recent increases in indirect taxes are likely to have had a regressive effect.

Soaring unemployment makes undergoing broad labour market reforms more pressing

The crisis has taken a heavy toll on employment, exacerbating the costs of long-standing labour market weaknesses. Pervasive segmentation keeps a high share of (mostly young) workers on short-term contracts, squandering human capital. Long-term unemployment is very high (Figure 10). Adjustment to downturns by reducing hours worked, rather than shedding workers, has traditionally been very low. Except for encouraging signs in the recent past, a decade-long rise in unemployment has failed to generate competitiveness gains through wage restraint. These problems are the joint outcome of defective settings in employment protection legislation, unemployment benefits, active labour market policies, and wage bargaining mechanisms.

Figure 10. **Unemployment developments over the past decade**

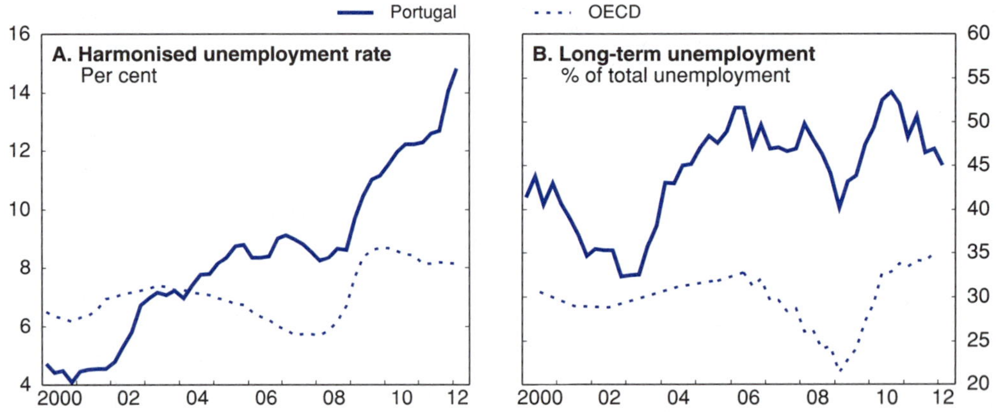

Source: OECD (2012), *Main Economic Indicators* (database), June and *Quarterly Labour Market Indicators Database*, Directorate for Employment, Labour and Social Affairs, April (unpublished data); OECD (2011), *OECD Employment and Labour market Statistics* (database) and Eurostat (2012), "Population and Social Conditions", *Eurostat Database*, June.
StatLink http://dx.doi.org/10.1787/888932669553

Shortcomings in wage setting mechanisms help to explain the difficulty in regaining competitiveness and the sharp rise in joblessness. They also stifle entry of new firms and competition in product markets. Wage bargaining mainly takes place at the sectoral level (Marques et al., 2009), where trade unions (which have the exclusive right to negotiate on the workers' side) and employers' associations (generally dominated by the largest firms) often account for only a modest share of total sectoral employment. These collective agreements are then administratively extended to whole industries (through the *portarias de extensão*), which gives extra clout to those sitting at the negotiating table and effectively stifles firm-level bargaining, thus hindering competition in labour and product markets

(Bassanini and Duval, 2006; Traxler et al., 2001). Further, upward pressures on wages were compounded by very strong minimum wage increases (5.3% per year on average in 2007-10, followed by a further 2.1% in 2011 despite a rapidly weakening economy). This has led to job losses for the low skilled (Centeno et al., 2011).

In welcome steps, the government agreed (May 2011) to freeze both the minimum wage and administrative extension, the former over the EU-IMF programme horizon (though with possible escape clauses) and the latter until clear criteria for extension have been defined. To promote firm-level bargaining, the authorities have also lowered the threshold for delegation of unions to work councils from 500 to 150 workers. Further, they committed not to extend any collective agreement subscribed to by employers' associations representing less than 50% of workers in a sector and, when that threshold is reached, to take account of the implications on competitiveness when deciding on extension. However, in May 2012 some pending requests for extension not complying with the 50% threshold were accepted, though with some postponement of the associated wage increases. While at a minimum the above commitments should be kept, the authorities should go further by keeping the minimum wage unchanged until there are clear signs of labour market recovery for low-skilled workers, and abolishing administrative extension altogether. The latter would further promote firm-level bargaining, fostering more dynamic labour and product markets.

Non-wage labour cost restraint could also help to smooth short-run adjustment and the associated employment losses. The authorities are implementing an increase in working time of up to seven days per year (as from 2013), coupled with more flexible working time arrangements (bank of hours), which decrease the need for overtime, and additional measures to reduce its cost. These reforms should lower long-run unit labour costs, improve competitiveness and facilitate future adjustment through hours worked rather than employment changes. In the short run, however, impacts on employment could be fairly muted. In contrast, reducing the labour tax wedge on low-skilled workers can yield sizeable employment gains (de Serres et al., 2012), especially given the high wage elasticities of labour demand in Portugal (Marques et al., 2009) and the past hikes in the minimum wage. Employment gains could materialise relatively quickly, especially for young people (OECD, 2012), while fiscal costs would be much lower than under a general cut in social contributions. The authorities should reduce employers' social contributions on low-wage workers on a permanent basis, to the extent that compensating measures can ensure compliance with fiscal targets. Though more expensive, an open-ended cut in contributions is likely more effective for employment creation than temporary marginal job subsidies, such as those recently introduced under the *Impulso Jovem* programme (targeted at long-term unemployed aged 18-30).

High employment protection on regular contracts and the ensuing labour market segmentation lower the sensitivity of wages to unemployment (de Serres et al., 2012) and harm firm performance and productivity growth, as the reallocation of insiders is hindered and outsiders under-invest in human capital (Centeno and Novo, 2012). The 2009 Labour Code reform, which mainly focused on reducing procedural inconveniences and notice periods for dismissals, still left Portugal with the highest protection for regular workers in the OECD (Figure 11), and with one of the largest gaps in protection between open-ended and temporary contracts. A new round of reforms, started in 2011, has succeeded in bringing Portugal closer to the OECD average. Individual dismissals grounded on job redundancy no longer need to follow a pre-defined seniority order, while those based on

Figure 11. **Strictness of employment protection legislation**
Scale from 0 (least stringent) to 6 (most restrictive), 2008

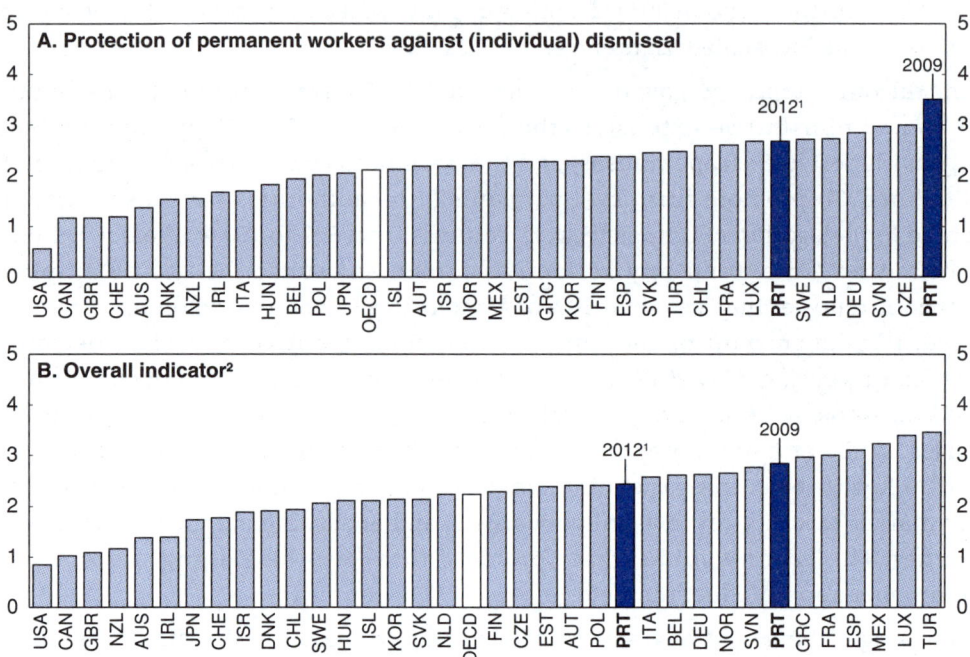

1. Based on changes to the Labour Code due to come into force in August 2012.
2. Weighted average of three sub-indices: protection of permanent workers against (individual) dismissal, regulation on temporary forms of employment and specific requirements for collective dismissal.
Source: OECD (2012), "Employment Protection Legislation", OECD Employment and Labour Market Statistics (database), July.
StatLink ▸ http://dx.doi.org/10.1787/888932669572

worker capability have become possible in a wider range of circumstances. Severance pay has been reduced from 30 to 20 days per year of tenure (with a 12-month ceiling instead of a 3-month floor) and existing contracts preserve entitlements accrued under the old rules (which minimises the risk of short-run negative employment impacts in the current difficult economic juncture).

Despite these significant reforms, employment protection for permanent workers remains above average (Figure 11). Given the weak performance of the labour market, more needs to be done. The authorities should further reduce severance pay, as envisaged under the financial assistance programme, and take additional steps to tackle labour market segmentation. The latter could include a longer trial period for open-ended contracts (currently 90 days for most workers) and, to reduce the high costs of litigation over dismissals, binding arbitration (entered into on a voluntary basis) as an alternative to courts, as envisaged. In the medium term, they could consider abolishing duality altogether by moving to a single employment contract.

The unemployment benefit system has long raised concerns as regards both labour market performance and social equity. Age-increasing benefit duration leads to high replacement rates for older workers (OECD, 2010a), whereas tight eligibility requirements have translated into narrow coverage of unemployment benefits, especially among young workers. The 2012 reform of unemployment benefits goes some way in addressing these concerns. Eligibility has been expanded by lowering the minimum required contributory period for unemployment insurance from 15 to 12 months and by extending benefit entitlement to self-employed workers who meet certain requirements. To tackle disincentives to work, the ceiling to unemployment insurance has been lowered by one sixth, a 10% benefit reduction applies after six months and under certain conditions jobseekers who take up a full-time job paying less than the benefit will be able to temporarily retain part of the latter. However, duration remains heavily age-dependent, as larger cuts in unemployment insurance duration for older workers are partly undone by longer provision of unemployment assistance (Figure 12). The effectiveness of reform is also hampered by a protracted phasing in. Benefit duration should not depend on age and should be shortened for older workers. The authorities should also assess whether changes to eligibility prove effective in improving benefit coverage, especially for young workers, and take further steps towards that aim if needed.

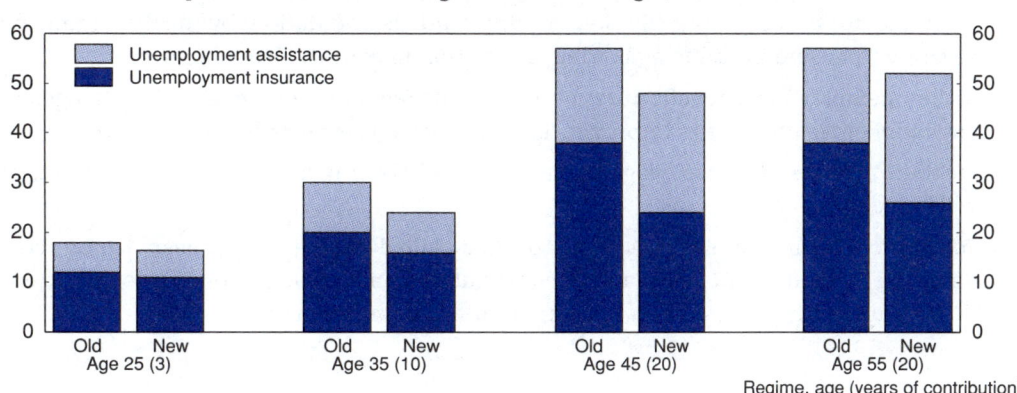

Figure 12. **Duration of unemployment benefits**[1]
Comparison of old and new regimes at different ages, duration in months

1. Unemployment insurance (*subsídio de desemprego*) and unemployment assistance (*subsídio social de desemprego subsequente*).
2. "New" concerns the regime since the 15 March 2012 reform (Decree-Law 64/2012). The number in parentheses represents the years of contribution since the last unemployment spell.
Source: OECD calculations based on Portuguese legislation.

StatLink http://dx.doi.org/10.1787/888932669591

Active labour market policies are important to keep jobseekers close to the labour market and, when needed, to help enhance their human capital. Job search assistance has substantial room for improvement in Portugal, via better targeting of resources, more outreach to employers and better use of available information on jobseekers and posted vacancies. Monitoring and sanctions, while very strict on paper (Venn, 2012), are in practice far less rigorous, as proof of job search is often undemanding and benefit cancellation is seldom applied.

The authorities should proceed with timely implementation of their recent programme for public employment service (PES) reform (*Programa de Relançamento do Serviço Público de Emprego*), which addresses some of the above weaknesses. Further, job search monitoring should be stepped up and sanctions made less stringent (*e.g.* a temporary reduction or suspension of unemployment benefit, rather than outright cancellation) but coupled with stricter enforcement. A recent job subsidies scheme, *Estímulo 2012*, will also help to keep job search requirements credible. Training programmes, which were significantly upscaled in 2008-10, should be streamlined, better attuned to participant characteristics and labour market skill needs, and designed so as to leave time for continued job search. This will be facilitated by the major analysis of active labour market policies currently being conducted. The "Vida Ativa" programme develops this approach, by shortening the duration between PES registration and the start of part-time training programmes. Moreover, the PES is recalling specific groups of subsidised unemployed, namely those aged 45 and above or unemployed for six months or more, to direct them to training or occupational programmes. On the youth front, the authorities are enlarging and modernising the dual learning system.

> **Box 4. Core recommendations to improve education, labour market and social cohesion**
>
> - Lift education levels by focusing the evaluation system more on tracking individuals and cohorts over time in order to inform policy changes to improve education outcomes of children from lower socio-economic backgrounds.
> - Continue to tackle labour market rigidity and segmentation by further reducing severance pay and introducing binding arbitration in conflicts over dismissals.
> - Make unemployment benefit duration not age dependent, and ensure that changes to eligibility prove effective in improving benefit coverage, especially for young workers.
> - Further promote firm-level wage bargaining by abolishing administrative extension of collective agreements.
> - To improve employment prospects for low-skilled workers and ease labour cost adjustment, reduce employers' social contributions on low-wage workers, to the extent that compensating measures can ensure that fiscal targets are met.

Progress in improving the business environment and product markets

Lifting Portugal's living standards in the long-run ultimately depends on raising trend productivity growth, which is low by international standards and especially compared with catch-up countries elsewhere in the OECD (Figure 13). Improving the business and product market environment is an important shorter-term avenue for achieving this. The government has taken a broad range of measures under the Simplex programme to improve the business environment by easing the licensing and permits system. Despite recent measures being launched, problems still exist at the local level, the civil justice system is inefficient and capital allocation is biased away from the tradables sector by excessive rents in non-tradables sectors due to insufficient competition and regulatory interventions.

Improving the legal framework
Steps to improve the justice system will benefit the whole economy

The justice system has been slow to resolve civil and commercial cases, resulting in an enormous number of pending cases (1.5 million) and particularly cases involving the enforcement of previous cases (1.2 million) (Intrum Justitia, 2011). This creates a high level of regulatory uncertainty for business, undermining investment and growth. To tackle inefficiencies in the justice system, the government is carrying out a wide-ranging reform including introducing a new insolvency law which entered into force in May and is designed to better facilitate corporate restructuring. Momentum in justice reform should be maintained with monitoring of whether the changes to the civil procedure code and insolvency laws in particular result in speedier civil and commercial case resolution. To

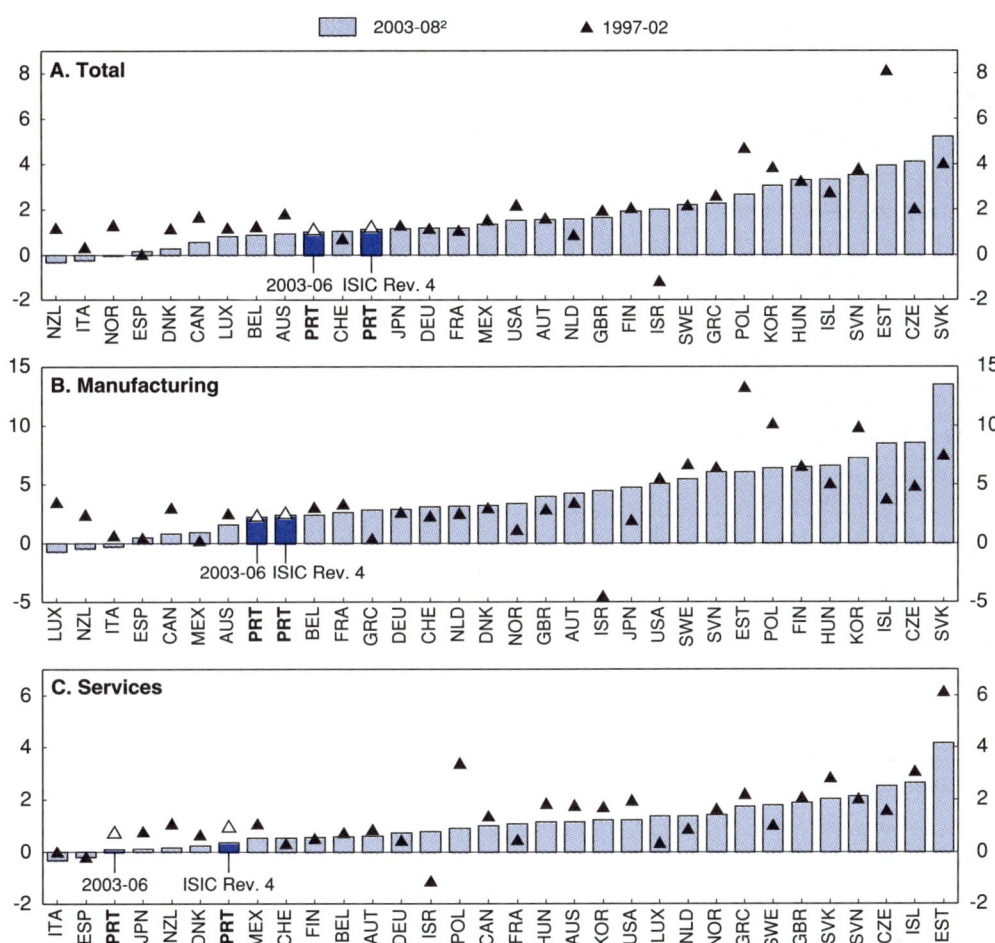

Figure 13. **Productivity growth by sector**[1]
Average of annual growth rates, per cent

1. Based on the International Standard Industry Classification Revision 3 (ISIC Rev. 3). To provide the best possible comparison and most recent data for Portugal both ISIC Rev. 3 and preliminary Rev. 4 data are shown. Between Rev. 3 and 4 the industrial classification was updated to reflect changes that have occurred in the structure and type of economic activity in recent years. Examination of limited ISIC Rev. 4 data available for other countries suggests that the change in classification has led to a general upward revision of productivity growth.
2. To 2006 for Australia and Portugal (ISIC Rev. 3); 2007 for Japan.
Source: OECD (2012), STAN: OECD Structural Analysis Statistics (database), April.

StatLink http://dx.doi.org/10.1787/888932669610

reduce regulatory uncertainty further, the government should improve the transposition of EU directives into Portuguese law by carefully considering local circumstances when legislating. This can help to reduce the need for subsequent legal amendments to remedy practical difficulties that arise because the law is ill-suited to deal with the local conditions, which creates uncertainty and delays for firms in the meantime.

Local licensing remains an impediment despite improvements

Although improving, local licensing is still a binding constraint on business generally. According to the World Bank's *Doing Business Survey 2012*, Portugal ranks 97th out of 183 countries, due to an excessive number of procedures and long times required to obtain the necessary municipal permits for construction. Reforms to speed up the process include allowing firms to directly make all the necessary applications (electricity, telecom, environment) to various agencies rather than relying on the municipality to coordinate this process, although some of the individual steps (*e.g.* fire safety) are still slow. This tends to work better for large well-resourced firms, which are more motivated to push their own application process rather than relying on the municipality, but small firms are likely to find this onerous.

The government is planning to carry out a more comprehensive "zero authorisation" reform in 2013. For firms of up to 20 employees industrial licensing would be automatic. The reform would also give municipalities a maximum of 60 days to consider an application for 98% of firms before approval must be given and most firms are expected to receive licensing within 30 to 40 days. For the remaining 2% of applications which are more complex and involve higher risks, it is intended to halve the current deadlines. This is a promising reform, which has the potential to substantially improve the business environment, and it should proceed without delay.

Efforts also need to be made to reduce costs. The direct cost of licensing fees is not high by international comparison but "surcharges" levied by municipalities before they give licensing approval can be up to one fifth of total development costs. As a high and uncertain implicit tax on new investment, these are a particularly distorting way to raise revenue. Following steps to reduce these surcharges in the "Zero Industrial Licensing" reform, the government should eliminate them and replace them with more stable and less distorting revenue sources for local government. The zero licensing initiative can potentially help reduce surcharges by reducing the scope for municipalities to delay granting a licence in order to extract these surcharges.

In the housing sector, a reform of the policies that excessively favoured homeownership and biased capital allocation is underway

Homeownership in Portugal has long been encouraged by rental market and tax policies, and, by 2011, 73% of dwellings were owner-occupied. These incentives, along with easy credit, led to a housing stock among the highest in the OECD area (557 dwellings per 1 000 inhabitants in 2011 of which 13% are vacant homes), excessive leverage of households and limited residential and labour mobility (Caldera Sánchez and Andrews, 2011). Cumbersome eviction procedures and long-standing rent controls for older contracts have inhibited rental housing supply and discouraged investment in dwelling maintenance. In this context, the new legislation on urban rental and the simplified regulations for renovation works are an important step forward. The authorities should ensure that the new eviction procedures, both through extrajudicial and judicial processes, effectively decrease the eviction time of non-complying tenants, as envisaged.

Recent changes in recurrent taxes on immovable property are welcome, including the on-going general update of the taxable value of urban properties and a significant reduction of temporary tax exemptions for principal owner-occupied dwellings. As the tax proceeds gradually increase, the real estate transaction tax should be levied only on the initial transactions of property, and in a second step could be replaced by VAT (OECD, 2010a). As regards personal income tax, the deductibility of mortgage interest payments is being gradually phased out and that of mortgage principal has been eliminated, which is welcome.

Strengthening competition to spur a more productive and innovative economy

Intensifying competition and improving the regulatory framework are important levers for raising Portugal's trend productivity, overall growth rate and cost-competitiveness. Insufficient competition in the non-tradable sector in particular has reduced overall productivity growth (Almeida et al., 2010). Greater competition is a potent force for boosting trend productivity and overall growth because it creates a permanent incentive for firms to be more innovative as well as putting pressure on them to lower costs and prices (Høj et al., 2007).

The regulatory framework plays an important role in ensuring effective competition. Portugal has improved over time and significant steps are being taken to further strengthen the framework. These include: relinquishing the government's "golden shares" in publicly listed companies that allowed it to block certain strategic decisions; major revisions to competition legislation; and introducing a new court specialised in competition issues. The changes to the competition law further align Portuguese legislation with EU law on merger control, increase the efficiency of the appeals process for competition law cases and extend the Authority's powers to carry out inspections and audits in the course of sector studies and antitrust actions.

The government should also ensure that a pro-competitive regulatory framework is in place before privatising assets that are in network industries (like transport) that are crucial inputs for other industries and have the potential to generate monopoly rents such as Aeroportos de Portugal (ANA). One possibility would be to involve the competition authority in the design of the sale and the regulatory framework. Another possibility would be to examine the case for dividing these assets up before sale to generate competition. The OECD's Competition Assessment Toolkit, which provides a flexible methodology for identifying legal and regulatory restraints to competition (OECD, 2011c) could be applied in Portugal to provide sector specific recommendations on the necessary regulatory changes to ensure assets sold in the privatisation programme operate in an environment that promotes competition.

The Toolkit could also be more broadly applied in improving the legal framework of the Portuguese economy, since it is designed to identify any type of policy, law and regulation that may unnecessarily impede competition, such as: i) restrictions on starting new businesses; ii) regulations that affect the ability of businesses to compete; and iii) regulations that affect business behaviour by changing the incentive of businesses to act as vigorous rivals. Once these are identified, the Toolkit can assist the government in assessing and revising those policies that do unduly restrict competition.

Despite positive development in the overall regulatory framework, market concentration remains high in important sectors of the economy and prices for some widely used inputs are still high by international standards. In addition several non-tradable sectors that already had high margins were able to increase them further during the 2000s (Amador and Soares, 2012). A common reason for this is that although there has been a high degree of legal liberalisation, other barriers to competition remain.

In the energy sector, addressing unwarranted returns in electricity is essential and competition in natural gas should be promoted further

Opening the electricity sector to private initiative and competition and promoting renewable energy have been at the core of Portugal's energy policy since the mid-1990s. The ownership of production is still highly concentrated on the previous incumbent and competition at the retail level is very limited (especially for households), while generation from renewable sources has increased to one of the highest levels in Europe (48% of gross electricity production in 2011), largely due to the rapid growth of wind power. Progress in harnessing renewable sources plays a major role in Portugal's contribution to the EU efforts to reduce greenhouse gas emissions and to strengthen energy security. Portugal's emissions have been declining in recent years and in 2009 were already slightly below its Kyoto Protocol target for 2008-12 (Figure 14). Energy policy objectives, environmental and other, have been largely pursued through generous support to producers. Most generators currently benefit either from feed-in tariffs (renewables and cogeneration) or from financial mechanisms to ensure profitability associated with the opening of the sector to private investment (fossil-fuel power and large hydro plants).

Figure 14. **Greenhouse gas emissions**
Index, 1990 = 100

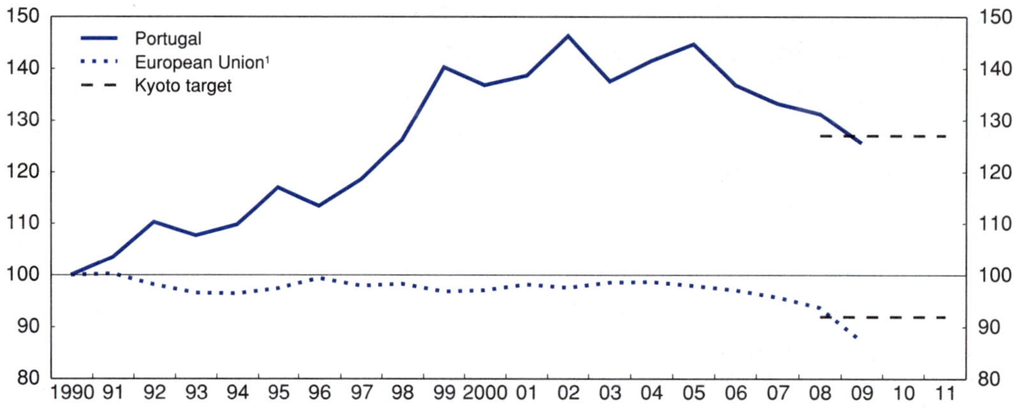

1. EU 15 member countries, i.e. before enlargement in May 2004.
Source: European Environment Agency and Eurostat (2012), "Environment and Energy", Eurostat Database, May.
StatLink http://dx.doi.org/10.1787/888932669629

The surge in wind turbine farms has increased electricity costs, through both feed-in tariffs and payments for availability, which reward the increased back-up standby of less intermittent generation. All costs of electricity generation support, either to renewables and cogeneration or to fossil-fuel power and large hydro plants, are supposed to be recovered through prices charged to end-users of electricity, with households facing in particular very high prices in international comparison. Still, prices for industry in 2011 were already above the OECD Europe average, according to preliminary estimates (Figure 15). However, the government has decided on several occasions not to fully transmit the costs to electricity prices, thus creating a significant tariff debt (EUR 1.8 billion at end-2011, about 1% of GDP), that is expected to be close to EUR 3 billion in 2012 and could increase further to around EUR 5 billion if no reforms were implemented. This crowds out credit to other sectors, as the debt has been securitised with banks, and poses pressure on future electricity prices.

The authorities must ensure that electricity generation support is made cost-effective and costs are fully passed on to all consumers. This requires reducing excessive supports to both wind farms and cogeneration, and to fossil-fuel power and large hydro plants. Under the EU-IMF programme commitment to eliminate the tariff debt by 2020, the authorities announced in May 2012 an intended reduction of overall support costs by around 1% of GDP over the quite long period 2012-20, but some measures are still to be legislated or negotiated with electricity generators.

Figure 15. **Evolution of electricity prices**
USD per megawatt hour[1]

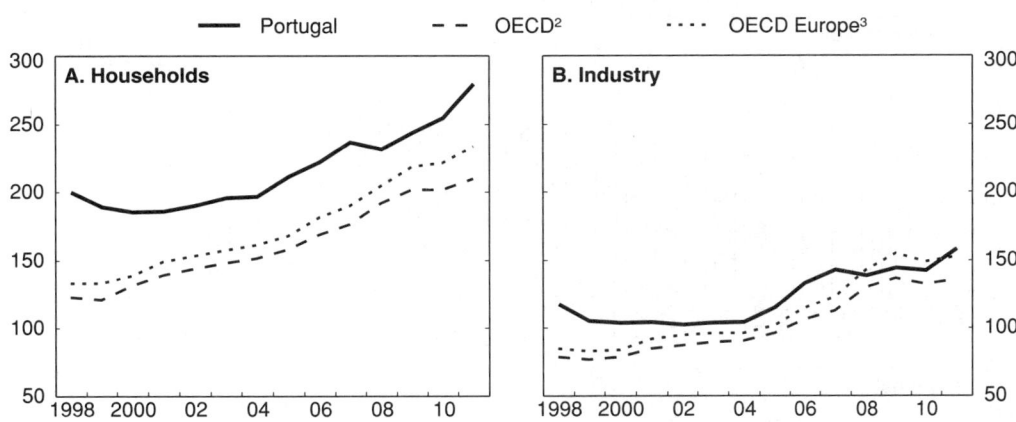

1. Total price in US dollars using purchasing power parities. The 2011 data for OECD and OECD Europe is an OECD estimate.
2. Unweighted average of 28 countries in panel A and 23 countries in Panel B.
3. Unweighted average of 20 countries in panel A and 16 countries in Panel B.
Source: IEA (2012), "End-use prices", IEA Energy Prices and Taxes Statistics (database), July.

StatLink http://dx.doi.org/10.1787/888932669648

In the case of wind farms, even though the most recent feed-in tariffs are consistent with those in other EU countries (OECD, 2011b), the authorities should reduce the costs stemming from the much higher tariffs still being paid to producers whose licences were not granted under tender mechanisms. As regards cogeneration, the authorities have already decided to reduce considerably their future remuneration. They should also introduce a time limit for feed-in tariffs for renewable cogeneration, as best practices recommend that incentives be transitional and decrease over time to foster technological innovation (IEA, 2008). In the case of fossil-fuel power and large hydro plants, the authorities should reduce the rates of return currently being guaranteed to the previous incumbent and to generators holding power purchase agreements, aiming at bringing returns closer to their average cost of capital. In addition, the government has already committed to redesign future payments for availability.

The importance of a cost-competitive natural gas supply in Portugal is growing due to new gas-fired electricity generation as well as greater industrial demand. Despite steps towards a liberalised market, wholesale and retail gas markets remain highly concentrated and prices are high by international comparison (Figure 16). Work on a joint Iberian gas market commenced in 2008 but it has been impeded by high cross-border transmission charges between Portugal and Spain. To encourage greater competition, the Portuguese energy regulator, in tandem with the Spanish energy regulator, should fully implement the recent inter-governmental agreement to reduce the cross-border transmission charges between Portugal and Spain to zero. Moreover, the incumbent, GALP Energia, owns exclusive contract rights to the supply of wholesale pipeline gas from Algeria, which is cheaper than sources available to competitors. The regulator should further require GALP to auction Algerian pipeline gas to other firms with no pre-set minimum price.

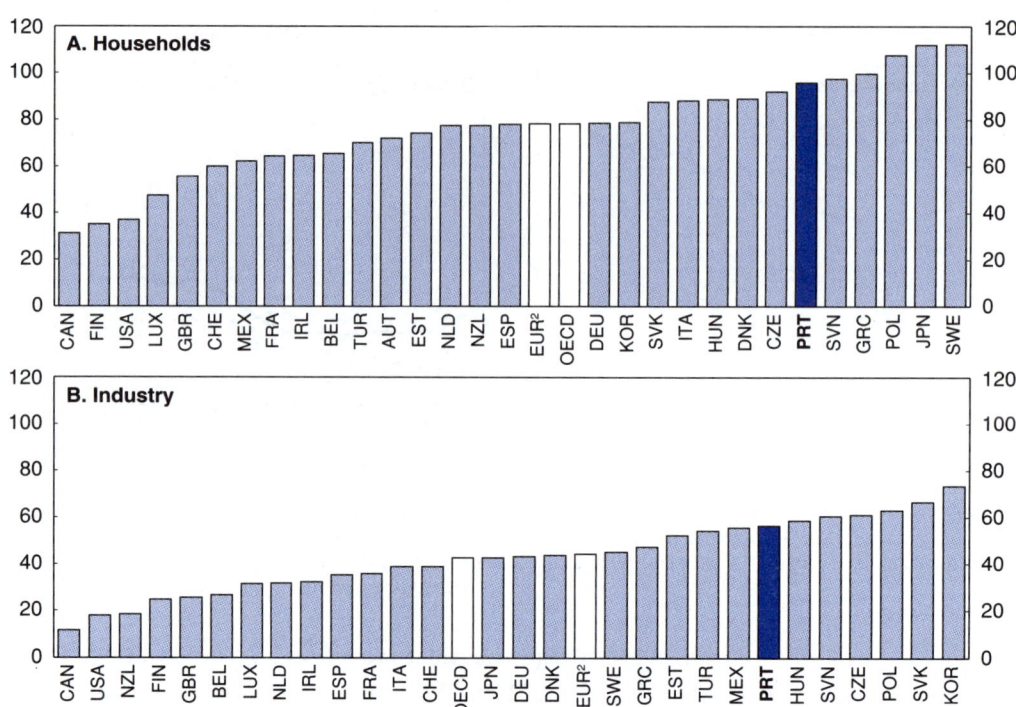

Figure 16. **Gas prices in international comparison**
USD per megawatt hour, 2010[1]

1. Total price in US dollars using purchasing power parities. In panel B 2009 for Denmark and 2008 for Mexico. The OECD and OECD Europe aggregates are unweighted averages of data shown.
2. OECD Europe.

Source: IEA (2012), "End-use prices", IEA Energy Prices and Taxes Statistics (database), July.

StatLink http://dx.doi.org/10.1787/888932669667

There is room to increase competition in telecommunications, the retail and wholesale sectors and professional services

There is evidence that competition in telecommunications is increasing in Portugal with market shares becoming generally more dispersed. However, from a country cost-competitiveness point of view, prices still appear relatively high for fixed line calls for business, leased lines used for connecting offices and branches, higher speed broadband internet and medium to heavy mobile phone usage (OECD, 2011d). With the rapid rise in the delivery of communication services via bundled services on mobile phones and other portable devices, greater competition in the mobile market would have benefits on several fronts. Mobile phone prices are still high by international comparison (Figure 17).

In a welcome move the telecoms regulator has lowered mobile call termination charges considerably, reducing the network advantages that firms with larger market shares have. To further level the playing field, origination charges for calls commencing on another network, which remain well above costs, should be reduced by regulation in line with termination charges as the costs of termination and origination are practically the same. Portugal should further facilitate competition by introducing a full Mobile Virtual Network Operator (MVNO) agreement allowing firms without a physical network to buy full wholesale access (i.e. voice, text messaging and internet) to the networks of the three existing physical networks at regulated wholesale prices.

Figure 17. **Mobile telephone prices in international comparison**
OECD basket including VAT, August 2010 (USD PPP)[1]

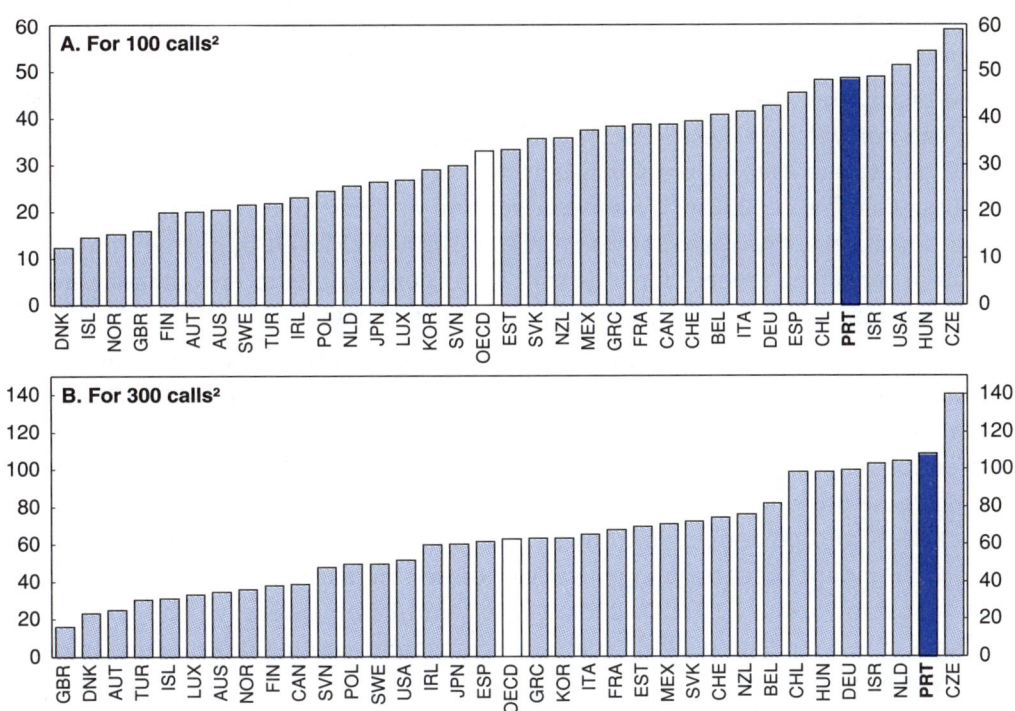

1. The OECD basket of mobile telephone charges covers subscription and usage over a one-month period (including value-added tax) and is shown in US dollars at purchasing power parities. Charges are distributed between peak and off-peak hours and are based on an average call duration. Tribal plans are not fully taken into account.
2. Voice calls including SMS messages: 140 SMS for 100 calls or 225 SMS for 300 calls.

Source: OECD (2011), OECD Communications Outlook 2011.

StatLink ⟶ http://dx.doi.org/10.1787/888932669686

Boosting competition to drive productivity improvements in the wholesale and retail sector has large potential pay-offs as it accounts for around 15% of total employment, and trend productivity growth in the sector has been among the lowest in the OECD. Although some of the distribution sector is composed of large modern retail and wholesale firms, the bulk of the sector is accounted for by small inefficient traditional enterprises, with average firm size very low compared with other European countries (OECD, 2010a). This likely lowers productivity as there is evidence of significant economies of scale in the retail sector (Nordás et al., 2008). Portugal also appears to be lagging in harnessing the benefits of e-commerce. Online shopping usage is very low by international standards (European Commission, 2010).

A broad mix of reforms is needed to improve competition in the distribution sector. Changes already made to sector specific regulations include an increase in the size thresholds for when extra rules and approvals apply to large stores, and liberalising opening hours regulation. These provide a good base on which to build further reform. Improvements to local licensing procedures, lower broadband prices to encourage e-commerce and liberalisation of rent controls would all help to create a regulatory environment more conducive to investment and productivity growth in the distribution sector. The new law on urban rental specifies that small businesses holding rental contracts prior to 1995 may benefit from a five-year transitory period, in which the ceiling for rent updating is often below current market values, a provision that distorts competition and is likely to cover many retailers. If a significant divergence between market and transitional regulated rents persists, the authorities should shorten the transitory period, raise the ceiling or adopt a narrower definition of small businesses.

The distribution sector, like others in the economy, would also be aided by labour market and port reforms. Restrictive employment protection legislation may have played an important role in keeping firms in this sector, as well as elsewhere in the economy, too small (Braguinsky et al., 2011). Greater competition at ports to lower transport costs and improve logistics in the distribution sector could be achieved by introducing a more transparent tendering process for renewal of port concessions to encourage more firms into the industry, which currently has little contract switching.

Professional services are an important input for many other sectors in the economy and also a potential source of export growth. Eighteen important professions including those in the accounting, architecture, engineering, health and legal fields are self-regulated by professional bodies. The government will introduce a new horizontal framework law requiring these professions to change their regulations to comply with the EU services, qualifications and selection directives. To enforce the law the government should introduce an independent regulator that can direct the associations to take regulatory action where necessary (OECD, 2007). This would help preserve the information advantages of self-regulation, while guarding against anti-competitive practices to restrict supply by the associations.

> **Box 5. Core recommendations on the business environment and product markets**
>
> - Maintain the momentum in justice reform to speed up civil and commercial case resolution.
> - Fully implement the proposed zero authorisation initiative to speed up local licensing.
> - Ensure that the new eviction procedures effectively decrease the eviction time of non-complying tenants in order to increase the supply of rental housing.
> - Introduce a full Mobile Virtual Network Operator (MVNO) agreement to increase competition in telecommunications.
> - Ensure that electricity generation support is made cost-effective and costs are fully passed on to all consumers. This requires further reducing excessive support to both wind farms and cogeneration, and to fossil-fuel power and large hydro plants.
> - Promote greater competition in gas markets by implementing the agreement with Spain to lower cross-border transmission charges to zero.

Bibliography

Afonso, A. and S. Fernandes (2003), "Efficiency of Local Government Spending: Evidence for the Lisbon Region", *Working Papers*, No. 2003/09, Department of Economics at the School of Economics and Management (ISEG), Technical University of Lisbon.

Ahrend, R., J. Arnold and C. Moeser (2011), "The Sharing of Macroeconomic Risk", *OECD Economics Department Working Papers*, No. 877, OECD Publishing.

Almeida, V., G. Lopes de Castro and R.M. Félix (2010), "Improving Competition in the Non-Tradeable Goods and Labour Markets: The Portuguese Case", *Portuguese Economic Journal*, Vol. 9, No. 3, Springer.

Amador, J. and A.C. Soares (2012), "Competition in the Portuguese Economy: An Overview of Classical Indicators", *Working Papers*, No. 8, Banco de Portugal.

Bassanini, A. and R. Duval (2006), "Employment Patterns in OECD Countries: Reassessing the Role of Policies and Institutions", *OECD Social, Employment and Migration Working Papers*, No. 35, OECD Publishing.

Braguinsky, S., L.G. Branstetter and A. Regateiro (2011), "The Incredible Shrinking Portuguese Firm", *NBER Working Paper*, No. 17265, National Bureau of Economic Research.

Caldera Sánchez, A. and D. Andrews (2011), "To Move or Not to Move: What Drives Residential Mobility Rates in the OECD?", *OECD Economics Department Working Papers*, No. 846, OECD Publishing.

Callan, T., C. Leventi, H. Levy, M. Matsaganis, A. Paulus and H. Sutherland (2011), "The Distributional Effects of Austerity Measures: A Comparison of Six Countries", *Research Note*, No. 2, Social Situation Observatory, European Commission.

Campos, M.M. and M.C. Pereira (2009), "Wages and Incentives in the Portuguese Public Sector", *Economic Bulletin*, Vol. 15, No. 2, Banco de Portugal.

Centeno, M., C. Duarte and A.A. Novo (2011), "The Impact of the Minimum Wage on Low-Wage Earners", *Economic Bulletin*, Vol. 17, No. 3, Banco de Portugal.

Centeno, M. and A.A. Novo (2012), "Segmentation", *Economic Bulletin*, Vol. 18, No. 1, Banco de Portugal.

Debrun, X., D. Hauner and M.S. Kumar (2009), "Independent Fiscal Agencies", *Journal of Economic Surveys*, Vol. 23, No. 1, Wiley Blackwell.

EPEC (2010), "Market Update: Review of the European PPP Market in 2010", European PPP Expertise Centre.

European Commission (2010), "Retail Services in the Internal Market. Accompanying Document to the Report on Retail Market Monitoring: 'Towards More Efficient and Fairer Retail Services in the Internal Market for 2020'", *Commission Staff Working Document*, COM(2010)355 final, European Commission.

Hagemann, R. (2010), "Improving Fiscal Performance Through Fiscal Councils", *OECD Economics Department Working Papers*, No. 829, OECD Publishing.

Haraldsson, G. and D. Carey (2011), "Ensuring a Sustainable and Efficient Fishery in Iceland", *OECD Economics Department Working Papers*, No. 891, OECD Publishing.

Høj, J.C., M. Jimenez, M. Maher, G. Nicoletti and M. Wise (2007), "Product Market Competition in OECD Countries: Taking Stock and Moving Forward", *OECD Economics Department Working Papers*, No. 575, OECD Publishing.

IEA (International Energy Agency) (2008), *Deploying Renewables: Principles for Effective Policies*, OECD Publishing.

IMF (International Monetary Fund) (2009), "The Economics of Bank Restructuring: Understanding the Options", *IMF Staff Position Note*, June 2009.

IMF (2012), "Third Review Under the Extended Arrangement and Request for a Waiver of Applicability of End-March Performance Criteria", *IMF Country Report*, No. 12/77, International Monetary Fund.

Intrum Justitia (2011), *European Payment Index 2011*, Intrum Justitia AB.

Kappeler, A. and M. Nemoz (2010), "Public-Private Partnerships in Europe – Before and During the Recent Financial Crisis", *Economic and Financial Report*, No. 4, European Investment Bank.

Marques, C.R., F. Martins and P. Portugal (2009), "Price and Wage Setting in Portugal", *The Portuguese Economy in the Context of Economic, Financial and Monetary Integration*, Economics and Research Department, Banco de Portugal.

Nordås, H.K., M. Geloso Grosso and E. Pinali (2008), "Market Structure in the Distribution Sector and Merchandise Trade", *OECD Trade Policy Working Papers*, No. 68, OECD Publishing.

OECD (2007), "Towards Better Regulation of the Legal Professions", background paper presented at the OECD Policy Roundtable on Competitive Restrictions in Legal Professions, June, DAF/COMP(2007)39, OECD Publishing.

OECD (2010a), *OECD Economic Surveys: Portugal 2010*, OECD Publishing.

OECD (2010b), *PISA 2009 Results: What Students Know and Can Do – Student Performance in Reading, Mathematics and Science* (Volume 1), PISA, OECD Publishing.

OECD (2011a), *Towards Green Growth: Monitoring Progress – OECD Indicators*, OECD Publishing.

OECD (2011b), *OECD Environmental Performance Reviews: Portugal 2011*, OECD Publishing.

OECD (2011c), *Competition Assessment Toolkit*, Vol. 2, *www.oecd.org/competition/toolkit*.

OECD (2011d), *OECD Communications Outlook 2011*, OECD Publishing.

OECD (2012), *Economic Policy Reforms 2012: Going for Growth*, OECD Publishing.

Pereira, M.C. (2010), "Educational Attainment and Equality of Opportunity in Portugal and Europe: The Role of School Versus Parental Influence", *Economic Bulletin*, Vol. 16, No. 4, Banco de Portugal.

Reis, R.F. (2012), "The Impact of PPPs Contracting on Portugal's Fiscal Position and What Can Be Done About It", presentation at the 5th annual OECD meeting on Public-Private Partnerships, March.

Santiago, P., G. Donaldson, A. Looney and D. Nusche (2012), *OECD Reviews of Evaluation and Assessment in Education: Portugal 2012*, OECD Publishing.

Serres, A. de, F. Murtin and C. de la Maisonneuve (2012), "Tackling Unemployment in a Weak Post-Crisis Recovery: Policies to Facilitate the Return to Work", *OECD Economics Department Working Papers*, OECD Publishing, forthcoming.

Sorbe, S. (2012), "Portugal: Assessing the Risks about the Speed of Fiscal Consolidation in an Uncertain Environment", *OECD Economics Department Working Papers*, OECD Publishing, forthcoming.

Traxler, F., S. Blaschke and B. Kittel (2001), *National Labour Relations in International Markets, A Comparative Study of Institutions, Change, and Performance*, Oxford University Press.

Veiga, L.G. (2010), "Determinants of the Assignment of EU Funds to Portuguese Municipalities", *NIPE Working Papers*, No. 11, Universidade do Minho.

Venn, D. (2012), "Eligibility Criteria for Unemployment Benefits. Quantitative Indicators for OECD and EU Countries", *OECD Social, Employment and Migration Working Papers*, No. 131, OECD Publishing.

ASSESSMENT AND RECOMMENDATIONS

ANNEX A1

Progress in main structural reforms

This table reviews action taken on recommendations from preceding Surveys. Recommendations that are new in this Survey are listed in the relevant chapter.

Past recommendations	Actions taken and current assessment
A. Fiscal policy and tax system	
Adopt a comprehensive medium-term expenditure framework supported by an expenditure rule.	Four year medium-term expenditure framework with a structural balance rule adopted.
Increase state-owned enterprises' (SOE) efficiency by expanding performance monitoring.	Quarterly reports published by the Ministry of Finance starting in 2009 Q1. Annual reports published since 2006. The role of the Ministry of Finance is being reinforced in the new legal framework, to be submitted to Parliament in June 2012.
Reduce the scope of the SOE sector by resuming the privatisation process if financial conditions permit.	Remaining shares in the former incumbent electricity generator, EDP, sold. A 40% stake in the electricity transmission owner and operator REN sold. Privatisation of TAP and ANA initiated.
Make the fiscal implications of public-private partnerships (PPP) transparent.	An accounting firm was contracted in February 2012 to provide a detailed report on PPP projects by June 2012.
Strengthen benchmarking across hospitals to improve efficiency. Ensure that hospitals are paid market level prices to help prevent systematic losses that would compromise them in supply negotiations and/or lead to higher input prices (2008 Survey).	Since 2011 reports are being produced comparing hospital performance on the basis of a set of monthly indicators.
Shift the tax burden from labour (especially low-skilled) to less distortive property or consumption taxes.	No progress on reducing the tax burden on labour. Additional revenue was raised by increasing the efficiency of the value-added tax (VAT) structure through the restructuring of VAT rates. Exemptions on annual property tax for owner-occupied dwellings were substantially reduced.
Reduce or eliminate expense-related tax expenditures (tax credits for education, mortgage interests and health care) and set pension allowances at the same level as for salary income.	The 2012 Budget reduced tax credits for health care, eliminated the deductibility of mortgage principal, eliminated interest income deductibility for new mortgages and phased out the deductibility of mortgage interest payments for owner-occupied housing and rents. In addition, pension allowances were reduced to the same level as salary income allowances.
Abolish inefficient corporate tax expenditures and promote base broadening.	Reduced corporate tax rates abolished and exemptions reduced in 2012 Budget.
Introduce an automatic expiry close for tax expenditures.	Tax benefits are subject to a sunset clause established in the Tax Benefits Statute.
Carry over a tax audit of independent workers.	The National Plan for Tax Audit 2012 sets independent workers as a priority group for tax audits in 2012.
Extend the scope of application of the standard rate of VAT.	The standard VAT rate was extended to gas and electricity from October 2011 and the 2012 Budget extended it from January 2012 to restaurants, more food products, as well as artistic and sports events.
Shift housing taxation from transactions to property. Increase property tax revenues by removing exemptions and regularly updating property values.	The 2012 Budget raised minimum and maximum rates for recurrent property taxes, introduced regular updating of property values. The general appraisal of 5.2 million urban properties was under way in June 2012.
Reduce the high tax compliance costs in cases of disputes and litigation.	A task force of judges was created to clear the backlog of cases with a value above EUR 1 million.
Enhance cooperation between tax and social security agencies by integrating agencies' databases.	A joint task force was established to enhance the exchange of information between the Tax Authority and the Social Security.

Past recommendations	Actions taken and current assessment
B. Labour market policy	
Reduce the contributing period to access unemployment benefits.	The minimum contributory period required for unemployment insurance has been lowered from 15 to 12 months.
Monitor the efficiency of the different entities supporting unemployed people.	Some progress in monitoring and assessing *Gabinetes de Inserção Profissional*, but with no policy implications so far. The recent Programme for Public Employment Service (PES) Reform envisages systematic performance assessment of job centres.
Make participation in training programmes compulsory after a specified duration of unemployment. Design training programmes to leave participants time for job search.	The authorities have been implementing measures broadly along these lines since February 2012, under the Programme for PES Reform.
To reduce labour market dualism, ease employment protection legislation (EPL) for regular contracts.	Protection for regular workers was partially reformed, especially in the areas of severance pay and dismissal rules.
Reform unemployment benefits to reduce their generosity for older workers and to make them decline with unemployment duration for all workers.	A 10% benefit cut after six months has been enacted. Some reduction in overall replacement rates, but there is only a modest shortening of total benefit duration (unemployment insurance plus unemployment assistance), which remains age-dependent and very long for older workers.
Improve flexibility in working-time regulations to allow larger adjustment of hours compared to employment.	Working time was made more flexible through "banks of hours" for individual workers or groups of workers, and overtime pay was lowered.
Encourage medium-term agreements between social partners to restore cost-competitiveness.	No progress.
C. Business environment	
Ease licensing procedures further, notably at the local level.	Introducing zero industrial licensing initiative that will make licensing automatic for 98% of firms after 60 days.
Reduce the length of the judicial process	New civil procedure code to be introduced to parliament in September 2012.
Further develop industrial clusters and cooperation between firms and R&D sector, but evaluate the effectiveness of such programmes.	No progress.
D. Transport infrastructure	
Resume the construction of the new Lisbon airport when financial conditions permit.	Project cancelled following a deterioration of financial conditions.
Reduce overreliance on road transportation through extended infrastructure user charges, *e.g.* tolls differentiated according to location, time and vehicle environmental efficiency, or smart parking pricing.	Higher tolls introduced on a number of roads.
Rationalise metropolitan public transportation and improve governance.	Legislation to change the way SOE managers are recruited and remunerated passed in January 2012. Legislation allowing the merger of operations of the Lisbon subway and the public bus operator has been approved, Merger is in progress and the boards of the two companies have been combined reducing combined board numbers from 10 to 4.
Ensure effective regulation of the new monopoly in the airport sector.	Work is underway to strengthen the competencies of the airport regulator.
Liberalise passenger railway transport activity.	No progress.
E. Education	
Enhance information on vocational education and training courses. Consider expanding the supply of apprenticeships.	Information on vocational and education and training courses is available from: the national qualifications authority (ANQEP) and *Mundo das Profissões* websites. Centres for Qualification and Vocational Education (former New Opportunities Centres) target youth who can go there for guidance. Education providers are being strongly encouraged to establish partnerships with firms in order to promote apprenticeships.
Reinforce evaluation tools to monitor the effectiveness of the *Novas Oportunidades* programme	Large scale programme evaluations were conducted, both from a lifelong learning (2010/11) and from an employability (2012) viewpoint.
Evaluate externally the effectiveness of the Educational Territories of Priority Intervention (TEIP) programme	An external evaluation conducted by two universities was completed in 2011.
Provide training to school managers and teachers to address increased diversity in the student body following the rise of the compulsory education age from 15 to 18.	No progress.
Systematically implement training for teacher evaluation within schools.	No progress.
Increase school autonomy to hire staff while also reinforcing accountability	No progress.
Give teachers financial incentives to work in difficult schools.	No progress. Not permitted under Portuguese law.
Reduce rates of school-year repetition and strengthen monitoring to reduce drop-out risks.	Revision of curricula and student support systems is underway. School level monitoring systems are in place and by law drop-outs must be reported.

Chapter 1

Solid foundations for a sustainable fiscal consolidation

> *Owing to slow growth and a relatively weak fiscal position, Portugal's public debt had been rising for almost a decade when the global crisis struck, sharply increasing the deficit. The loss of confidence in Portuguese and other euro area sovereign bonds required international financial support. Weak fiscal performance reflects a wide range of fiscal structural problems resulting in poor control of expenditure. At both the central and local levels, this was compounded by the non-transparent accumulation of payment arrears, future spending obligations via public-private partnerships (PPPs) and off-balance sheet debt in state-owned enterprises (SOEs). In line with the EU-IMF programme, the government is steadfastly implementing an ambitious front-loaded consolidation plan underpinned by a wide range of structural reforms. In a context of weak private sector demand, the government's ability to regain control over public debt dynamics depends crucially on avoiding spending overruns. This will require reinforcing the fiscal framework to improve expenditure control, tackling payment arrears and avoiding further negative surprises from loss-making SOEs, PPPs and local governments. The success of the programme will also require maintaining social consensus around it, notably through continuous attention to its implications for the poorest. If growth is far lower than projected in the programme, the automatic stabilisers could be allowed to operate at least partially to reduce the risks of a deeper recession and higher unemployment.*

Introduction

Portugal has a long record of fiscal deficits. In the past two decades, the fiscal deficit never fell significantly below 3% of gross domestic product (GDP), despite resort to one-offs to improve headline figures. This situation, combined with weak growth, resulted in a gradual but sustained rise in public debt since 2000. In 2009, debt increase shifted to a much steeper path as the deficit deteriorated dramatically to 10.2% of GDP (Figure 1.1). Rising debt, weakening growth prospects and turmoil in the euro area led to a loss of investor confidence and access to long-term market finance at sustainable interest rates. Portugal entered an European Union-International Monetary Fund (EU-IMF) financial assistance programme (hereafter referred as the programme) in May 2011.

This chapter discusses Portugal's fiscal situation and progress in dealing with the underlying drivers of the weak fiscal position. The first section analyses the risks around debt sustainability, and how consolidation should be designed to minimise harm to medium-term growth and maintain public support for the programme. This is followed by a discussion of the fiscal framework including measures to improve expenditure control. A final section covers efforts to deal with the large off-balance sheet liabilities and inefficiencies built up in state-owned enterprises (SOEs), public-private partnerships (PPPs) and local government and with the use of EU structural funds.

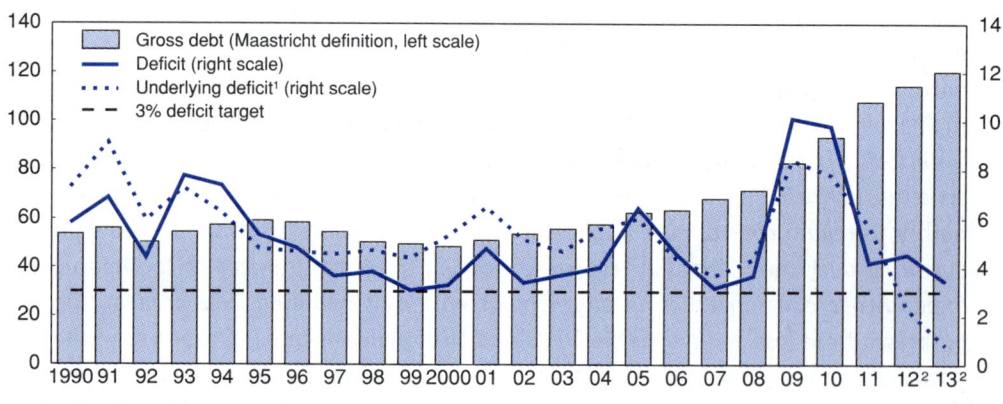

Figure 1.1. **Long-run fiscal indicators**
Per cent of GDP

1. Cyclically adjusted less one-offs.
2. Projections.
Source: OECD (2011), *OECD Economic Outlook: Statistics and Projections* (database), May.
StatLink http://dx.doi.org/10.1787/888932669705

The consolidation programme: how fast and with which instruments?

The speed of consolidation and risks around achieving debt sustainability

The government aims to reduce the public deficit to 4½ per cent of GDP in 2012 and 3% in 2013 as part of the EU-IMF programme, and projects the public debt ratio to peak at 116% of GDP in 2013 and then start declining (Table 1.1). Due to the need to make up for the large

Table 1.1. **Stability programme targets and assumptions**
Per cent of GDP[1]

	2010	2011	Targets and assumptions				
			2012	2013	2014	2015	2016
Public balance	**-9.8**	**-4.2**	**-4.5**	**-3.0**	**-1.8**	**-1.0**	**-0.5**
Expenditure	51.3	48.9	47.5	45.9	44.6	43.8	43.0
Revenue	41.4	44.7	42.9	42.9	42.8	42.7	42.5
Public debt (Maastricht definition)	93.3	107.8	113.1	115.7	113.4	109.5	103.9
Real GDP growth (%)	1.4	-1.5	-3.0	0.6	2.0	2.4	2.8

1. Revenue and balance include a number of one-offs of which the most notable is a positive one in 2011 of 3½ per cent of GDP corresponding to the transfer to the government of the assets of banks' pension funds, in exchange for overtaking future pension liabilities.
Source: OECD (2012), OECD Economic Outlook: Statistics and Projections (database), May for historical series of 2010-11 and Ministry of Finance (2012), Documento de Estratégia Orçamental 2012-16 for targets and assumptions of 2012-16.

one-offs in 2011, such targets will require a large underlying fiscal consolidation of about 3½ per cent of GDP in 2012 – almost twice as much as in 2011 – and about 1½ per cent of GDP in 2013. Under the OECD's central scenario of a gradual economic recovery beginning in 2013, the ambitious fiscal stance envisaged by the authorities would allow to rapidly regain control over public debt dynamics. However, there are risks of a deeper than projected recession, notably because of the ongoing credit contraction (Chapter 2). First data for 2012 show a budget deficit of 7.9% for the first quarter on a seasonally unadjusted basis because of lower indirect tax revenues and higher social transfers. In such a case, the question is whether the government should stick to nominal deficit targets, which risks further amplifying the recession and being potentially self-defeating, or let automatic stabilisers play, which would delay public debt stabilisation, with a risk to investor confidence.

Stochastic simulations carried out by the OECD illustrate the trade-off between sticking to nominal deficit targets and letting automatic stabilisers play in an uncertain macroeconomic environment (Sorbe, 2012), (Figure 1.2). These simulations rely on a small-sized stylised macroeconomic model inspired by Lenain et al. (2010), in which random shocks affect macroeconomic variables following the approach developed by Celasun et al. (2006). The model captures the mutual interdependences between the fiscal position, financial conditions and activity and notably the impact of public debt developments on investors' confidence and interest rates. The fiscal multiplier, which has a large influence on the results, is assumed to be one – a level that would be considered rather high in normal times, reflecting that depressed private demand and tight credit may amplify the impact of fiscal consolidation (Corsetti et al., 2012).

The simulation results suggest that sticking to nominal deficit targets would put debt on a declining path, but with a significant risk of a deep recession and an associated sharp rise in unemployment. In this case, meeting nominal deficit targets would require large additional consolidation measures, which would risk undermining social support for the programme in a context of high and rising unemployment. In contrast, letting automatic stabilisers play would limit the risk of an extreme recession, but at the cost of abandoning certainty over debt control. On balance, this suggests that the government should aim at meeting its nominal fiscal targets (without resorting to one-offs) as long as growth does not deviate substantially from the programme to reap the associated credibility gains.

1. SOLID FOUNDATIONS FOR A SUSTAINABLE FISCAL CONSOLIDATION

Figure 1.2. **Stochastic simulation results**

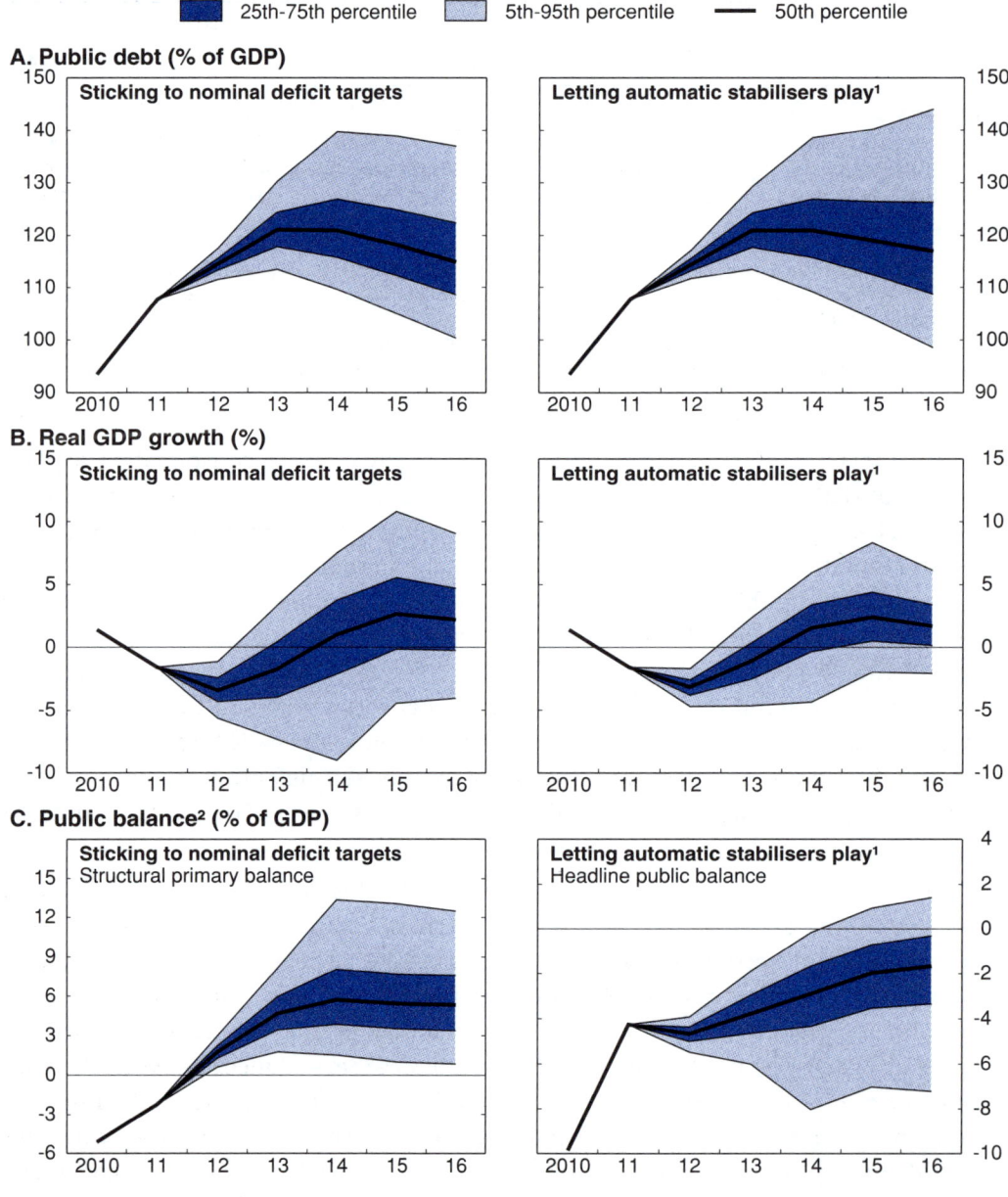

1. Respecting the structural primary deficit targets.
2. In the "nominal targets" strategy, the headline public balance is always equal to the targets presented in Table 1.1. Similarly, in the "automatic stabilisers" strategy, the structural primary balance always follows targets implied by the programme.

Source: S. Sorbe (2012), "Portugal: Assessing the Risks about the Speed of Fiscal Consolidation in an Uncertain Environment", *OECD Economics Department Working Papers*, forthcoming.

StatLink ⟶ http://dx.doi.org/10.1787/888932669724

Nevertheless, should output fall substantially more than projected, the automatic stabilisers should be allowed to play, at least partially. Debt simulations also show that risks around the fiscal consolidation programme would be minimised by stimulating potential growth through structural reforms (Chapter 2) and by choosing "growth friendly" fiscal consolidation instruments that would lower the fiscal multiplier (Annex 1.A1).

Consolidation instruments, growth, equity and the environment

After a fiscal stimulus of around 1% of GDP in late 2008 and 2009, as part of the European economic recovery plan, Portugal resumed fiscal consolidation in 2010 that gathered pace in 2011 and 2012. Two-thirds of measures in 2011 and 2012 are on the expenditure side, largely through reductions in the public sector wage bill via staff reductions as well as cuts in public sector wages. In addition the indexing of pensions to inflation was suspended except for the lowest pensions. In early July 2012 the Portuguese Constitutional Court ruled that the suspension of the 13th and 14th months paid to civil servants and pensioners through to 2014 (accounting for approximately 1.1% of GDP of the consolidation package for 2012) violated the constitution because it does not apply to all citizens. Given the country's deficit target commitments, the Court has nonetheless accepted that the suspension, as currently defined, can be applied in 2012. The government is currently analysing the possible alternatives scenarios to incorporate the Court decision into the budgetary plans beyond 2012. On the revenue side, amongst other measures, a personal income tax surcharge was imposed on higher incomes (those in the highest tax bracket), the state surcharge on corporate profits was increased, social security contributions were raised and value-added tax (VAT) increased both by lifting the main rate and abolishing a concessionary rate on electricity and many other items in 2012 (e.g. restaurants). Tax expenditures have been further reduced by cutting and capping tax allowances for health, mortgage and rent expenditure and abolishing all concessionary corporate tax rates. User charges including road tolls and public transport fares have been increased.

Consolidation instruments should be chosen so as to ensure a lasting improvement in the fiscal balance, minimise negative effects on activity, spread fairly the burden of adjustment across the population and, when relevant, help preserve the environment. In this respect, on the one hand, concentrating consolidation measures on the expenditure side would have a stronger negative effect on short-run activity as the impact of expenditure cuts is generally considered higher than tax increases (OECD, 2009a). On the other hand, international experience shows that expenditure based consolidations tend to be more successful, notably in terms of sustainability (Guichard et al., 2007).

On balance, the government will need to rely on both tax increases and expenditure restraints. Relying on the least-distortive taxes will minimize the short-term cost of the adjustment. From that perspective, the current consolidation package has a number of attractive features including raising revenue through indirect tax increases (Arnold, 2008), broadening the tax base through reducing tax expenditures rather than raising tax rates, and harmonising tax rates by suppressing certain concessionary rates. However, consolidation should put greater weight on expenditure measures since excessive growth in expenditure has been the main source of poor fiscal performance. In times of fiscal restraint, the emphasis should be on improving spending efficiency, notably concerning SOEs and local governments, and, as has been the case, on cutting current rather than capital expenditures as short and medium-term negative growth effects are lower.

The burden of adjustment needs to be spread fairly to maintain social consensus around the programme. In particular, continuing attention should be paid to its implications for the poorest. By design, the reduction of certain tax credits, public sector pay cuts and income tax changes have affected high income earners more, having clauses to protect the lowest income brackets. However, consolidations tend to have adverse impacts on income distribution (Ahrend et al., 2011). Recent research suggests that (excluding increases in indirect tax other than VAT and cuts in public services), between 2009 and mid-2011, Portugal's package may have been more regressive than in five other EU countries examined (Callan et al., 2011). Indeed, the combined effect of the measures considered in this study reduced disposable incomes of the two lowest income deciles in Portugal proportionally more than those of higher income deciles, mainly as a result of pension and benefit cuts which hit the poorest harder.

The decision to impose tolls on formerly free highways is welcome as it raises revenue while also benefiting the environment. The government is also planning, in tandem with municipalities, to develop a package of measures to promote the use of public transport. Measures include extending bus lanes as well as increasing parking restrictions and the cost of individual transport. The last is particularly welcome as planned metro price increases would otherwise lead to passengers moving to other, more polluting, transport forms. The authorities should be ambitious in this area, by for example widening the coverage of and increasing parking fees, introducing congestion charges in Lisbon and making greater use of road tolls. This would even up the competitive playing field between metro, rail and individual road transport, help to reduce pollution and congestion, provide a source of funding for public transport and increase market efficiency by bringing user costs closer to the social costs of individual road transport. Tolls should be set as a part of a wider transport strategy that takes into account the environmental costs as well as the overall costs and revenues arising from all transport state-owned enterprises including the rail companies.

Improving the fiscal framework

Portugal has a relatively poor record of achieving its budget targets, especially medium-term ones, largely owing to a failure to adequately control expenditure. With the exception of the 2005-07 consolidation, public expenditure has been allowed to rise more rapidly than GDP since 1998, when Portugal's entry to the euro was confirmed, undermining the fiscal position (Figure 1.3). The failure to control expenditure is partly a result of over-optimistic economic and revenue forecasts, which is a widespread source of budgeting problems (OECD, 2011a), and assumptions on capital revenue (Figure 1.4). It also reflects spending overruns, compounded by a failure to minimise risks arising from local and regional government, the state-owned enterprise sector and public-private partnerships, as discussed below.

A stronger fiscal framework would help to solve these problems. By enhancing credibility, it can also help to reduce the need for sharp fiscal corrections that increase volatility of GDP growth in the short-run, which in turn undermines the economy's long-run growth rate (Brzozowski and Siwinska-Gorzelak, 2010). Portugal is overhauling its fiscal framework via the Budget Framework law of May 2011 and subsequent legislation. The main elements include: a medium-term framework of budget planning that annually sets expenditure ceilings for the central government for the next four years (November 2011); a general government budget balance rule in line with European level requirements to have a structural deficit of no more than 0.5% of GDP (after a transition period until 2014, during which the government will follow the programme targets); establishing an independent

1. SOLID FOUNDATIONS FOR A SUSTAINABLE FISCAL CONSOLIDATION

Figure 1.3. **Fiscal policy phases and breakdown of current expenditure**
Change in percentage points of GDP, annual average[1]

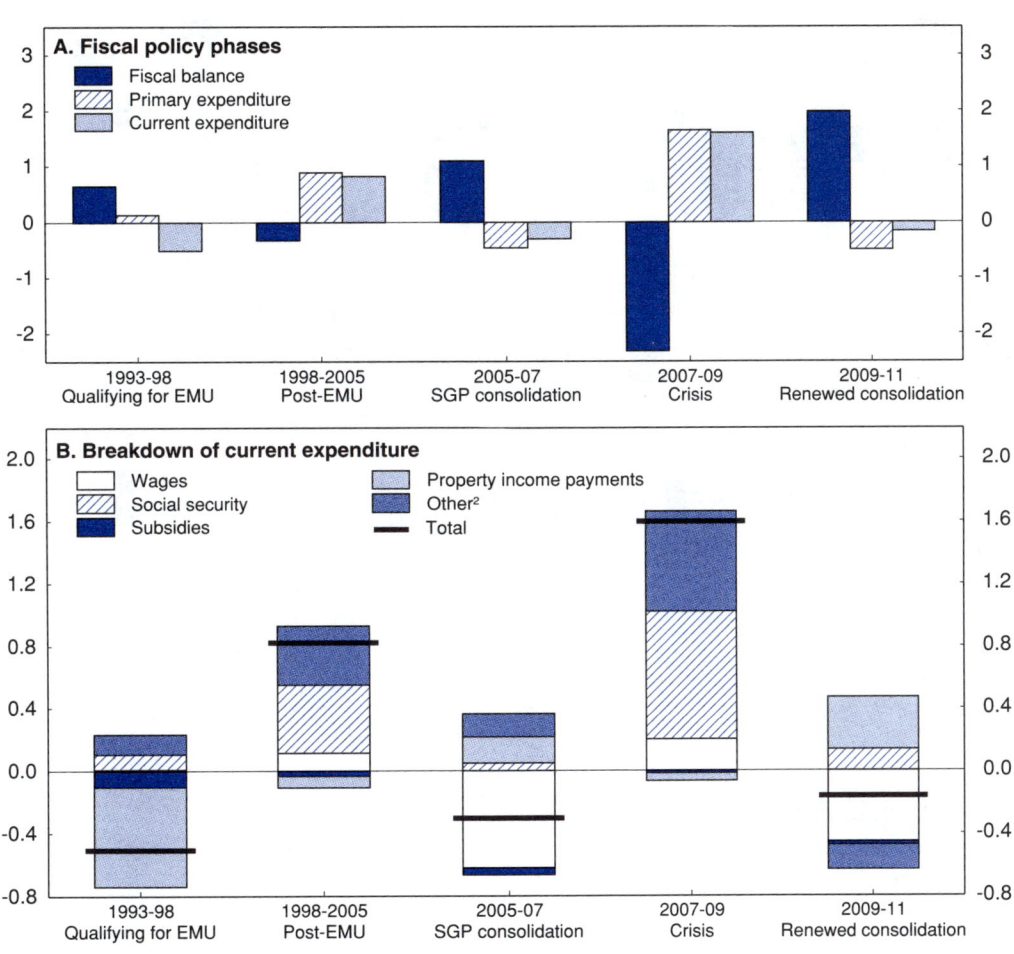

1. Based on national accounts definition. EMU: Economic and Monetary Union; SGP: Stability and Growth Pact.
2. Non-wage expenditure and other current payments.
Source: OECD (2012), OECD Economic Outlook: Statistics and Projections (database), May.
StatLink ⟶ http://dx.doi.org/10.1787/888932669743

fiscal council (October 2011); programme budgeting; and expanding the State Budget to the whole of general government as defined in the national accounts. Reforms of regional and local finances laws will also be presented before the end of 2012.

While implementation challenges still lie ahead, the new framework is a major step forward and is consistent with international best practice. Notably, the move towards a more medium-term focus is welcome given that Portugal has hitherto been relatively weak in this area by international standards (OECD, 2011a). However, ensuring that the framework really contributes to fiscal sustainability will require meeting important implementation challenges. In addition, the framework would be more transparent and easier to monitor if it were reinforced by a spending rule consistent with the structural balance rule and the new European fiscal framework. An expenditure rule is easy to monitor, addresses directly a major weakness of Portuguese fiscal policy, and would help to guide fiscal consolidation by providing an overall expenditure envelope within which to plan programmes.

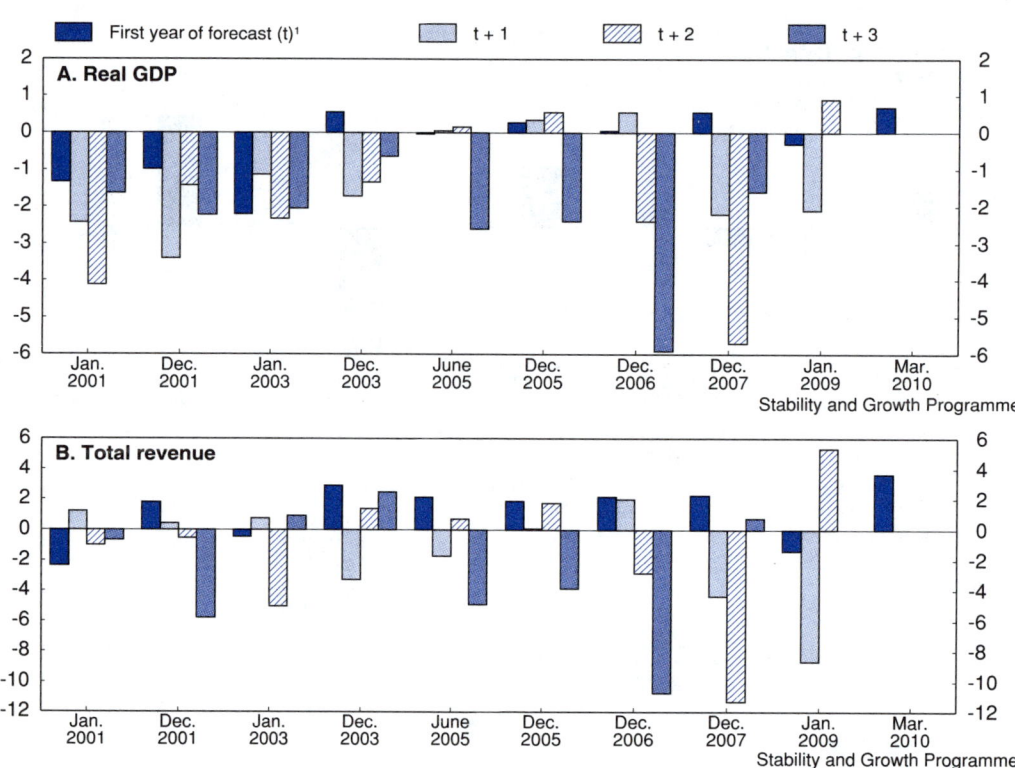

Figure 1.4. **Forecast errors for real GDP and general government revenue**
Actual growth less projections from Stability and Growth Programmes, percentage points

1. The first year of forecast is the same year as that of the programme except for the following: December 2001 t = 2002, December 2003 t = 2004 and January 2009 t = 2008.
Source: Portuguese Republic (1998-2010), *Stability and Growth Programmes* and OECD (2012), *OECD Economic Outlook: Statistics and Projections* (database), May.

StatLink ⟶ http://dx.doi.org/10.1787/888932669762

Budget control and financial management

The new framework will only be effective if the government is able to implement its budget plans and prevent slippages (Figure 1.5). In the past, inadequate monitoring has undermined the government's ability to achieve its targets, as evidenced by the generation of various contingent liabilities and payment arrears, as well as the frequent need to pass supplementary budgets to cover expenditure overruns despite the existence of a central budget contingency fund. Spending control efforts are hampered by the highly fragmented nature of financial reporting even at the central government level. Over 500 individual central government spending units report to the Ministry of Finance. The detailed monitoring and control of so many spending units leaves very little resources for the Ministry of Finance to get an overall view of individual ministries and major spending areas and therefore exercise effective budget control (OECD, 2008a).

Fragmentation of reporting has been amplified by an incomplete accounts reporting system. Reporting has been long, confusing and often repetitive. In addition, the accounts are cash based and have not used the same definition of the general government as that used in the national accounts produced by the National Statistics Institute (Ministry of Finance, 2011a). The Ministry of Finance has also in the past not had sufficient information about the sources of potential liabilities including SOEs and PPPs (particularly at the local

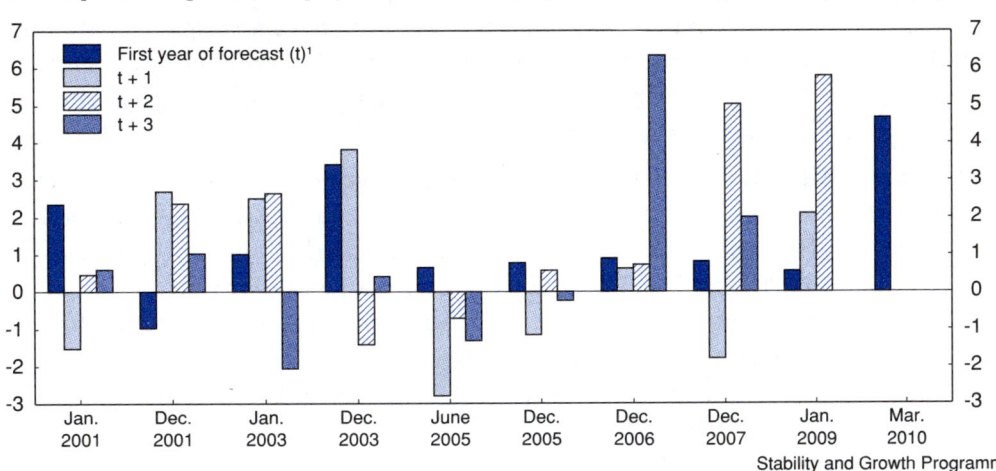

Figure 1.5. **Expenditure growth forecast errors**
Actual expenditure growth less projections from Stability and Growth Programmes, percentage points

1. The first year of forecast is the same year as that of the programme except for the following: December 2001 t = 2002, December 2003 t = 2004 and January 2009 t = 2008.
Source: Portuguese Republic (1998-2010), Stability and Growth Programmes and OECD (2012), OECD Economic Outlook: Statistics and Projections (database), May.

StatLink ⟶ http://dx.doi.org/10.1787/888932669781

level) and local and regional government finances on a sufficiently frequent basis (OECD, 2008a). Additionally, data on health spending and local and regional government accounts was previously only available quarterly. This has prevented the government from being able to get a timely picture of the overall general government position and risks to it.

Information flows are improving. The move to monthly reporting for all parts of general government is welcome. The broadening of the reporting universe in the State Budget to all entities included in the general government will also help the monitoring of the overall state of the government sector and improve international comparability. The government also plans to overhaul the accounting system, moving to a set of accrual based accounts containing results that can be compared across expenditure areas, which is welcome. More recently the Ministry of Finance has produced annual and quarterly reports on SOEs and PPPs at the central government level and some basic financial and operational information about individual SOEs is also provided. In addition, in line with programme requirements, the government produced a range of new reports including ones covering arrears, the 36 most important PPP contracts as well as 24 concessions. This excluded the PPP programme in the autonomous region of Madeira, which ran into serious difficulties in 2011 with one of the three PPPs in the region having been reclassified within general government resulting in fiscal implications at the general government level.

As recommended by the 2008 OECD Review of Budgeting in Portugal, the government is moving towards a programme budgeting approach. The State Budget will be structured around 14 programmes, each with a single implementing ministry. Also in line with OECD Budgeting Review recommendations, each minister will be responsible for strict compliance with the budgetary limits set for their respective ministry. Importantly, ministers will be liable for correcting any shortfall and failure to do so will result in lower budget allowances in the following year. In addition, each minister has appointed a programme financial controller to interact with the Ministry of Finance in monitoring and controlling budget implementation (Ministry of Finance, 2011a).

The move to programme budgeting will help tackle the problem of fragmentation and assist the Ministry of Finance to move away from detailed control of budget execution, which should reside with individual ministries, towards more strategic global oversight and reviews of financial performance. Programme budgeting will also complement the new medium-term expenditure framework discussed below by providing a better system for ensuring spending remains within the framework limits.

Once programme budgeting is fully embedded, the government should move towards improving performance information. A new OECD index shows that Portugal has a relatively under-developed budget performance information system by international standards (OECD, 2011a). Initial efforts should concentrate on developing a small set of internationally comparable output and outcome indicators that can be monitored over time against benchmarks in key expenditure areas such as health and education. This information can be used to go beyond just controlling expenditure within set limits but assist in reallocating expenditure to increase efficiency.

It is also important that the authorities fully implement the new system of intra-annual expenditure commitment controls based around the 14 new budget programmes. In the past, spending slippage occurred because spending units were allowed to spend excessively on the basis of over-optimistic forecasts of their own revenues, while no corrective action was taken when these revenues failed to materialise. The new system aims to remedy this. If spending exceeds the forecast revenue envelope in a three month period, this will have to be offset by more ambitious spending targets to correct this over the budget year. A potential issue is that the technical capability of programme financial controllers to carry out these oversight functions and interact with the Ministry of Finance varies a lot across other ministries. To instil a greater sense of responsibility, financial controllers should be appointments assigned to named individuals rather than simply a function assigned to the head of the planning unit for example. In addition, they should have sufficient time to properly carry out these functions and have access to analytical support staff, which is not the case for all ministries.

Further efforts are also needed to reduce payment arrears. Arrears of the general government sector, as well as the SOEs outside the general government sector, are high by international standards. The 2011 European Payments Index showed that the average payment delay by the public sector was the fourth highest out of 25 countries (Intrum Justitia, 2011). In early 2012, total arrears including those of SOE hospitals were around 3.2% of GDP. Controlling arrears is important as they are part of government debt in the wider sense (although they are not directly accounted in Maastricht debt) and, are a burden on private sector capital resources and thus on economic activity. The 2012 Supplementary Budget allocated EUR 1.5 billion (0.9% of GDP) for the settlement of existing arrears for the hospital sector, which is expected to be paid out by August. To prevent the build up of new arrears in 2012, the government has concentrated on providing adequate allocations to the health sector, where around 40% of the arrears have been concentrated. In addition, incentives are built into the newly introduced commitment control system to pay back arrears, as entities with spending arrears are forced to adopt more ambitious spending targets. The government has also committed to help local governments settle part of their existing arrears via a EUR 1 billion (0.6% of GDP) credit line, as discussed below.

Medium-term budgeting and anchoring the framework

Medium term budgeting has been insufficient, as Portugal was ranked second lowest on this issue out of 30 OECD countries in 2007 (OECD, 2009b; OECD, 2011a). This ranking takes into account a set of variables including the presence of multi-year expenditure estimates in the annual budget. The government's move to a comprehensive medium-term expenditure framework is therefore welcome. The medium-term expenditure framework can help to improve transparency in fiscal policy by showing how targets will be achieved as well as the multi-year consequences of spending and revenue plans. The latter restricts the scope to use expenditure shifting across years to hide unfavourable trends.

In the new framework, the government has committed to submit to parliament annually expenditure ceilings for the following four years. In the first year (the budget year) these ceilings will be expressed by the individual 14 programmes, for the second year they will be grouped by policy intervention areas, while only an overall ceiling will apply for the third and fourth years. The government should extend the period of individual programme ceilings beyond the first year. The extended ceilings could in addition be linked to specific measures, thereby giving the framework more credibility. The medium-term expenditure framework should be part of a broader medium-term economic and fiscal plan. Such a plan should include estimates for expenditure and revenue year by year and the specific measures that will be used to achieve targets. It is also important that the assumptions underpinning the plan are transparently laid out to give it credibility and allow effective monitoring by the Fiscal Council, the Parliament and the wider public.

Fiscal rules

In the same way as an annual budget, a medium-term expenditure framework can be adjusted every year, which limits its scope to discipline fiscal policy decision making. Thus, fiscal rules would be a useful complement that could be used to enforce the framework and achieve a medium-term fiscal target. They may also help to increase financial market confidence in the government's commitment to its medium-term plan. However, a poor track record of compliance with fiscal rules so far (the Stability and Growth Pact) means that the latter benefit may take some time to materialise for Portugal.

Recent and on-going decisions at the EU level in the context of the euro sovereign debt crisis have increased the number and overall strictness of common fiscal rules. There is now a complex web of four partially overlapping rules: the excessive deficit rule that requires the deficit to be below 3% of GDP; a debt convergence rule requiring the gross debt in excess of 60% of GDP to be reduced on average by at least 1/20th per year; an expenditure rule which constrains expenditure to increase by no more that the growth of potential GDP (with a lower reference rate for countries with a structural deficit below the medium-term objective – benchmark is a structural deficit of no more than 0.5% of GDP) unless there are explicit revenue raising measures; and a structural balance rule to reduce the annual structural deficit to below 0.5% of GDP in steps to be determined by the European Commission. In the case of Portugal these steps are already pre-determined through to 2014 by the EU-IMF programme.

Which rule is the binding constraint depends on circumstances, but recent EU communication has mainly focused on the structural balance rule (see European Council, 2011), which Portugal has enshrined in the new 2011 Budget Framework law. The new rule will apply from 2015 with the programme targets governing the path for the fiscal balance up until 2014. Rules should tackle as directly as possible the underlying source of the weak fiscal position (Sutherland et al., 2012), which in the case of Portugal is a failure to control primary expenditure (Hauptmeier et al., 2011). Rules also need to be not unduly rigid (Schick, 2010), easily understood and monitored by the parliament and public, have broad coverage and be operationalised easily. On this basis, Portugal should also legislate an explicit expenditure rule that limits public expenditure growth relative to the estimated growth rate of potential nominal GDP (as estimated *ex ante*), and use this to set enforceable nominal expenditure ceilings for general government to facilitate monitoring.

Historical experience suggests countries with multiple rules have been more successful in carrying out consolidations and stabilising debt (Guichard et al., 2007; IMF, 2009; Sutherland et al., 2012). Concerns about over-determining fiscal policy with multiple rules can be mitigated by parameterising such a numerical expenditure rule to be consistent with the structural balance rule obligation – the change in the balance being approximately equal to the difference between the growth rate of expenditure and potential nominal GDP weighted by the expenditure share in GDP.[1] With the current need to consolidate the fiscal position, this would require setting expenditure growth below potential nominal GDP growth for many years, which would be in line with the EU level expenditure rule obligation.

An expenditure rule provides a way of making the structural balance rule operational because performance against the expenditure rule can be judged against a simple observable target, expenditure, whereas the structural balance cannot be observed, but only estimated, with estimates typically revised significantly over time. Experience elsewhere suggests that the ease of observing compliance becomes an important issue in practice. For example, the Swedish Fiscal Policy council found it difficult to assess compliance with the government's target of a 1% surplus over the cycle (Calmfors, 2010). Disputes over when the cycle started and finished were among the most contentious aspects of the "over the cycle" rule that operated in the United Kingdom until the end of 2008 (OECD, 2009c). The potential gains from an expenditure rule are demonstrated by simulations showing that, if Portugal had followed this type of rule from 1999 to 2009 using real time data and limited primary expenditure growth to an estimate of potential nominal GDP growth, the debt-to-GDP ratio would have been 17 percentage points of GDP lower by 2009 (Hauptmeier et al., 2011).

Establishing a fiscal council

A fiscal council can complement fiscal rules by providing a body to assess whether the government is complying with them. A council can also help to give flexibility to fiscal rules and suggest improvements to them (Calmfors and Wren Lewis, 2011). In October 2011, the government passed legislation establishing an independent fiscal council. This is welcome, as it will bring independent, intellectually rigorous scrutiny to fiscal policy. The Council comprises five senior council members of which two may be non-Portuguese citizens, as well as a secretariat of analytical support staff. The board members were appointed by the end of 2011 with analytical staff appointments taking place in 2012. A first report was issued in May 2012, focusing on the broad aspects of the government's budgetary strategy (Portuguese Public Finance Council, 2012). The Council's main recommendations were for the government to hand over responsibility for macroeconomic forecasts to an independent institution and, as recommended in this *Survey*, set expenditure ceilings for general government.

The Council has a very wide remit. In addition to what are becoming standard tasks for these institutions internationally of assessing central government macroeconomic and fiscal forecasts and compliance with fiscal rules, the Council also has responsibility for assessing the financial position of local governments and state owned enterprises and analysing existing commitments including, pensions, health care, public-private partnerships and tax expenditures. The government is required by law to provide to the Council in a timely manner all economic and financial information it requires to complete its mission. The law also requires the Council's reports to be sent to the President of the Republic, the government, the parliament, the Court of Auditors and the central bank. The Council is a complementary fiscal institution to the Parliamentary technical budget support unit (UTAO) set up in 2006. In this context, it will be important to ensure regular information exchanges with this unit. The design of the fiscal council has already drawn on this unit's experience and should continue to do so, particularly in interacting with the parliament which will be a key client of the Council.

The provision to allow for up to two non-Portuguese citizens on the board will widen the range of perspectives. However, the government should relax the prohibition on board members having other paid activity. Other countries allow board members to hold concurrent positions and the prohibition is a serious constraint on recruitment where some of the potential candidates could be academics or economists in policy organisations who would be reluctant to fully give up their current jobs.

The Council's broad remit appropriately recognises that fiscal problems at the general government level can often arise outside the central government as has occurred in Portugal in recent years. However, it will be important to ensure resources available to the Council are commensurate with its wide remit. The Council will require significant analytic and specialised resources to meet the challenge of giving advice across such a broad range of areas. In the first instance the Council should prioritise core functions, including assessing the macroeconomic and fiscal projections, compliance with fiscal rules and giving fiscal policy recommendations to the government. Assessing the forecasts is an important task as international experience shows that over-optimistic macroeconomic forecasts are a notable source of deficit bias (Hagemann, 2010). Furthermore, there is evidence that Fiscal Councils that provide policy recommendations rather than just analysis are more effective (Debrun et al., 2009). Concentrating efforts will also help the Council to establish a reputation for high quality non-partisan work and therefore cement its role in the national debate and policy process.

Giving the Council strong power to request information from the government is also welcome, as limited access to important fiscal information has reduced the effectiveness of councils elsewhere (Kopits, 2011). The Council's role should be further embedded in the policy debate by requiring the Minister of Finance to provide a formal response, including appearing before the Parliamentary Finance Committee, to Fiscal Council reports. Finally, the Council should engage early in developing communication channels, particularly with the media which are the main channel of influence of the Council as it can only persuade and not coerce (Kopits, 2011).

The budgetary process provides only short periods for scrutiny of the Budget (OECD, 2008a). This is inconsistent with OECD guidelines on budget transparency (OECD, 2002), which suggest that the parliament should have three months to scrutinise the budget rather than the current one and a half months. This meant that the Parliamentary technical budget support unit (UTAO) had only ten calendar days to analyse the State Budget and eight days for the Stability Programme annual update. This constraint will also affect the new Fiscal Council as there have been no changes to extend the parliamentary timetables to approve the budget. Given the complexity of the budget and the severe implications of mistakes, the government should extend the time available to the Fiscal Council to analyse and report on the budget beyond that which was available to UTAO. This will help to ensure the Council can properly fulfil its functions.

Public sector efficiency and off-balance sheet liabilities

Raising the game of the SOE sector

Although previous privatisations have reduced the size of the state-owned enterprise (SOE) sector, in 2010 it still accounted for 4.5% of GDP and 3.5% of employment (DGTF, 2011a), (Figure 1.6). The corporatisation of a high proportion of hospitals partly explains this, as they represent more than half of SOE employees. More recently restructuring in the SOE sector has seen staff levels decline in areas such as the transport sector where personnel declined by 12% in the second half of 2011. The poor performance of the SOE sector overall is illustrated by the EUR 1.9 billion (1.1% of GDP) loss by the sector in 2011 on total assets of EUR 55.8 billion (32% of GDP). Poor performance of enterprises classified inside the general government sector, which account for most of the losses, directly affects the government's accounts. Those located outside general government represent a contingent liability, which may move on budget in the case of their reclassification to the general government sector or trigger a need to support them with debt guarantees or capital injections.

Figure 1.6. **Employment in state-owned enterprises**
Employees in SOEs in per cent of total employment, 2009[1]

1. Or latest year available. State-owned enterprises (SOEs) cover firms that are majority owned by the government or those where the government owns at least 10% of the common share capital listed.
Source: H. Christiansen (2011), "The Size and Composition of the SOE Sector in OECD Countries", OECD Corporate Governance Working Papers, No. 5.

StatLink ⏵ http://dx.doi.org/10.1787/888932669800

Many SOEs have been financially underperforming. Losses have been large in the urban passenger transport, rail and hospital sub-sectors (Figure 1.7). This partly reflects extremely high debt and associated debt servicing costs. Several of these companies are technically insolvent and the SOE sector as a whole has negative equity of EUR 2 billion. Nearly all of these loss-making companies (Carris, a public transport company, is an exception) are also making losses on an EBITDA (earnings before interest taxes, depreciation and amortisation) indicating that they are also operationally weak.

Figure 1.7. **State-owned enterprise performance**
By industry/company, in million euros at end 2011[1]

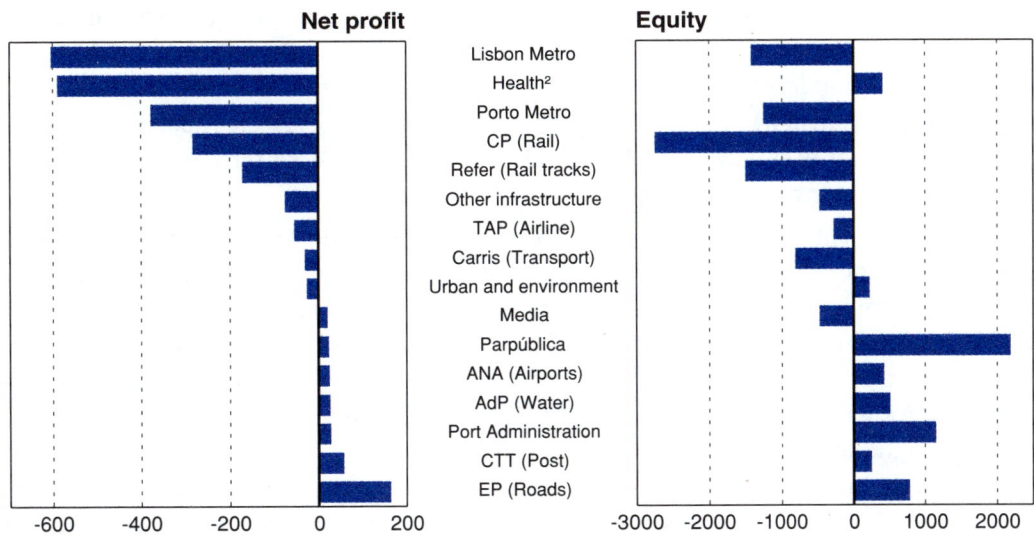

1. 2010 for TAP.
2. Losses in the health sector include those of a new hospital whose revenue was not fully recorded in 2011.
Source: Ministry of Finance (2012), Boletim Informativo Sobre o Sector Empresarial do Estado: 4.º Trimestre 2011 and Parpública (2011), Documentos de Prestação de Contas 2010.

StatLink ⇒ http://dx.doi.org/10.1787/888932669819

The reclassification by Eurostat of three SOEs as part of the general government sector has increased the urgency of solving these problems as their losses now have an immediate impact on the fiscal balance and debt. The reclassified companies are among the largest loss making SOEs (the rail track company, REFER, and the Lisbon and Porto metro companies), adding around ½ per cent of GDP to the fiscal deficit between 2007 and 2010 (Statistics Portugal, 2011; Ministry of Finance, 2011b). Occasional capital transfers from government to SOEs have been used to prop up ailing enterprises and prolong this process. However, experience shows this former strategy is not sustainable in the medium-run as Eurostat will reclassify particularly bad loss making enterprises as part of the general government sector, in which case the liability is immediately made explicit.

Running SOEs at a loss in sectors such as urban transport and health care and building up off balance sheet liabilities, including in the case of hospitals through payment arrears, reflected a non-transparent subsidisation of government services. In the short-run, lower priced but potentially inefficient services are delivered to the population without recognising explicitly the associated public cost. Alternatively, the debt of the SOE may become so large that it does not have enough free cash flow to pay suppliers and creditors and therefore to operate commercially. Operating the SOE sector in this way has also had negative externalities in the form of creating government guaranteed debtors that crowd out private sector borrowing and investment (Chapter 2).

Both the operation of SOEs and the policy framework that surrounds them should continue to be reformed. At issue are which enterprises the government should continue to own and how the performance and governance of these remaining companies can be improved. Part of the programme conditions are to privatise a number of enterprises including Aeroportos de Portugal (ANA), the national airline (TAP), the national postal service, Correios de Portugal (CTT), railway freight branch (CP Cargo), the insurance arm of a government bank (Caixa Seguros). The sale timetable is ambitious, with all of these assets programmed to be sold by early 2013. By mid-2012, the government had already executed the partial sale of REN and the sale of its remaining stake in the former electricity generating incumbent (EDP) and initiated the sale of ANA and TAP. The government had also announced that it intends to grant concessions to run the newly merged Lisbon metro and road public transport services companies as well as rail services. A partial sale of the television channel (RTP) along with a concession to run the water company Águas de Portugal (AdP) is being considered.

With the exception of the airline, TAP, the companies that are to be sold are profitable, which should increase the chances of prompt sales. In addition, they are engaged in commercial activities that the private sector can be expected to provide. The government should prioritise maximising the contribution to Portugal's long-term growth potential from the sale of these assets over a quick sale, especially at a time of crisis, when conditions for asset sales may not be the best. In any case, these are complex assets operating in industries where a healthy competitive market cannot be taken for granted due to natural monopoly characteristics and other barriers to entry. This means that a straight sale of these assets risks transforming public monopolies into private ones, with no real possibility of competition entering the market. An important part of privatisation will therefore be to ensure that the company structure and the regulatory framework are pro-competitive prior to any sale. For example, the government should consider splitting some of these firms into competing companies before selling them, even if this may delay sales. The government should also involve the competition authority in the design of the sale and the regulatory framework.

In terms of operational performance the government is developing a strategy for all SOEs with commercial activities (excluding the rail track company REFER and the health sector) to achieve operational balance by the end of 2012. Part of this are plans to reduce operational costs by at least 15% through decreasing the cost of supplies, external services and labour (DGTF, 2011a). The elimination of the 13th and 14th month salaries for all public sector employees including those in SOEs plays a major role in the latter. In the short-run redundancy costs resulting from cuts in staff will temporarily slowdown improvement. Despite this, data for the first quarter of 2012 point to an improvement in the operational balance of many SOEs compared with the previous year.

The losses of the Lisbon and Porto metro companies are so large that they are noticeable at an overall government budget level, with a combined net financial loss of EUR 980 million (0.5% of GDP) in 2011, of which more than half represented an operational loss. For the Lisbon metro a fundamental problem is that payments to suppliers and particularly staff have been increasing faster than sales revenue. From 2005 to 2010 staff payments rose by 18% and revenue from sales only rose by 7%. To prevent further deterioration in operational results, payments to staff will need to be far more tightly controlled. The Porto metro has had more success in cutting supplier costs and operational revenue coverage of costs improved between 2009 and 2010. To help close the gap between revenue and costs further, prices were significantly increased (by around 20%) for urban public transport in 2011 and the government's strategy is to increase them over time to comparable EU levels.

The national rail track company, REFER and the national operator of train services, Comboios de Portugal (CP), are also making large operational losses. Durably improving their operational performance may require further rationalising networks by closing underutilised and unprofitable lines and replacing them with bus services (where these are viable). Indeed, most of CP passenger's past operational losses have been incurred by CP regional in providing only 20% of CP's total available seat kilometres. Train services should only be provided on lines with high traffic density as the large fixed costs incurred in providing rail services mean the combined costs of CP and REFER per passenger kilometre rise drastically as total passenger kilometres on a line fall. On this basis, four lines were closed in 2009 and replaced with bus services that can be provided at a small fraction of the cost of train services (Ministry of the Economy, 2011). From 2011 through to mid 2012 a further 410 kilometres of underperforming parts of the network were deactivated. The government should continue to rationalise the network to eliminate remaining high cost lines to further reduce operational losses. Improving CP operational performance would also give more scope to raise infrastructure charges paid by the freight operation (scheduled for privatisation) to REFER and thereby reduce the losses of REFER.

Currently the revenue REFER earns from train operators is far below the costs of providing rail infrastructure and does not even cover staff costs. By international comparison, REFER's charges for utilising and managing infrastructure are below average overall and particularly for freight (Figure 1.8). A constraint on improving the bottom-line are EU network access pricing rules which prevent REFER from raising track access charges to recover the large investment costs it has incurred in recent times to modernise the network. The company has announced it wants to reduce losses through a 35% cut in staff and also other expenses in 2012. To help ensure this cost cutting is sustainable the government should continue to close the most unprofitable tracks in tandem with the rationalisation of train services by CP.

Figure 1.8. **Rail infrastructure access charges**
Euro per train kilometre, 2008[1]

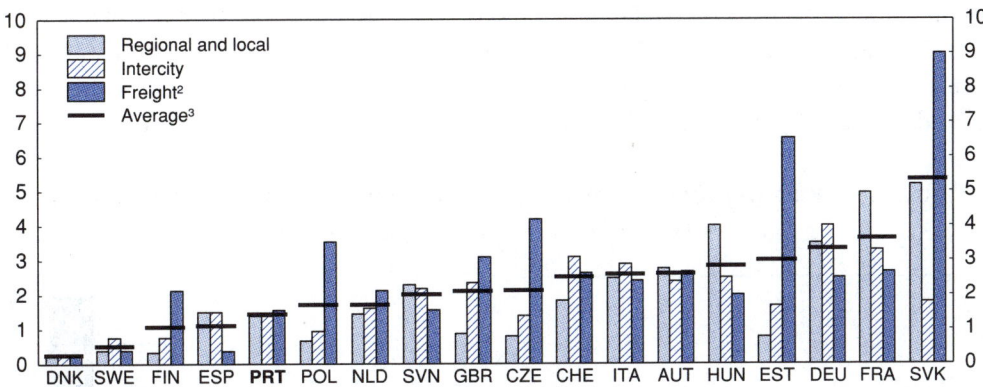

1. 2007 for Poland.
2. For a 960 ton freight train.
3. Unweighted average.
Source: OECD (2008), Charges for the Use of Rail Infrastructure 2008, International Transport Forum.
StatLink http://dx.doi.org/10.1787/888932669838

However, cutting costs and raising prices may not close the financial gap of certain public transport companies, meaning that they would have to rely on subsidies. This may be economically justifiable as those travelling on public transport generate positive externalities relatively to travelling by car. Nevertheless, in line with *OECD Guidelines on Corporate Governance of State-Owned Enterprises*, it is important that this subsidy is explicitly set and shown in the government's accounts in return for an agreed level of services, rather than via an accumulation of non-transparent losses. The public transport companies should be required to achieve at least operational balance after subsidies under such an agreement or face immediate corrective actions to restore balance.

Even if operational balance is achieved in loss making SOEs, the legacy of past recurrent losses has left them with a heavy debt burden that will continue to hinder financial performance. In some cases the debt has reached such high levels that it cannot easily be repaid. To put these SOEs back in a commercially viable position, their debt needs to be reduced to serviceable levels while avoiding future moral hazard through a better governance regime. The government is preparing a plan to tackle the debt burden issue that is due in July. To ensure this process is transparent the government should consider a one-off transfer of part of SOE debt to a government entity charged with repaying it from government revenues assigned to this entity for this purpose.

The government is introducing a new legal framework for SOEs and has plans to improve SOE governance. A new law changing the way SOE managers are recruited and remunerated was passed in January 2012 and further reforms are planned. A draft law to be considered by the parliament and applying to central and local SOEs envisages a new technical unit to monitor SOEs and to *inter alia* advise *ex ante* on whether establishing new SOEs is in the public interest. The government's plan to ensure the new framework also tackles the capability and authority of SOEs to enter into derivative contracts is welcome as a large contributor to the losses of the metro companies is from bets on interest rate derivatives which should have been used exclusively as a hedging tool.

Public-private partnerships have created a significant future drain on fiscal resources

From 1990 to 2010 Portugal was the third biggest user of public-private partnerships (PPPs) in Europe, after the United Kingdom and Spain and the highest user relative to GDP (Kappeler and Nemoz, 2010; EPEC, 2010; Figure 1.9). Accumulated investment in PPPs increased from EUR 9.3 billion in 2005 to EUR 16.2 billion (9.5% of GDP) in 2011 (DGTF, 2011a). As elsewhere in continental Europe, the vast bulk (79%) of these projects were roads, with rail (18%) and health (2%) accounting for most of the remainder (Kappeler and Nemoz, 2010).

Figure 1.9. **Public-private partnership contracts reaching financial close**[1]

Contracts for 1990-2009 as a percentage of 2011 GDP[2]

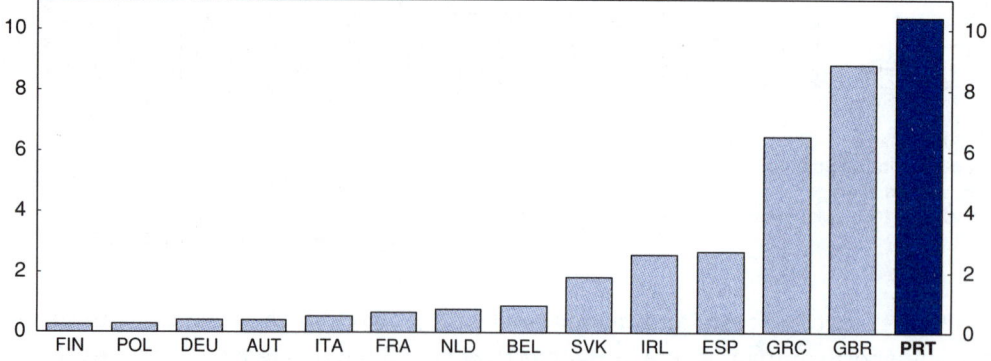

1. Financial close: project contract and financing documentation is signed.
2. The Czech Republic, Hungary and Sweden are not shown as their share is less than 0.02%.

Source: A. Kappeler and M. Nemoz (2010), "Public-Private Partnerships in Europe – Before and During the Recent Financial Crisis", *Economic and Financial Report*, No. 2010/04, European Investment Bank and OECD (2012), *OECD Economic Outlook: Statistics and Projections* (database), May.

StatLink http://dx.doi.org/10.1787/888932669857

Concerning roads, a variety of private-partnership models were introduced in three main waves (Table 1.2). Estradas de Portugal (EP), a 100% state-owned company that is classified within general government, is the government's principal road concessionaire. EP has in turn granted sub-concessions to private partners. In 2010 and 2011, the government negotiated with private partners to convert all the "shadow" toll roads – where the government paid tolls on behalf of users – to standard toll roads where users are charged a toll. This resulted in reclassification of the road investment as part of the general government expenditure because the tolls paid by users to the government are greater than 50% of the availability payments made to the private sector by the central government. In essence the central government is carrying most of the risk in the project and therefore the road is treated as a public asset.

Table 1.2. **Road sector public-private partnership models**

Model	Road length (kms)	Payments	Notes	Principal government risks
Wave 1: launched late 1980s. Private concession from the government (tolls paid by users).	1 300	Private partner bears the costs of running the highway and obtains the toll revenue.	After 2028 these assets will progressively move to Estradas de Portugal (EP).	Limited, but returns conceded to the private sector are very high.
Wave 2: Launched end 1990s. Private concession from the government. Seven shadow tolls paid by the government on behalf of users, highways now converted to EP sub-concessions with user tolls.	900	Originally: EP made payments to private partner and no user toll. Now: EP makes availability payments to keep the road open in good condition to private partner. State receives tolls collected by the private partner from users.	Tolls introduced in 2010 and 2011. These assets will eventually move to EP.	Demand risk.
Wave 3: launched 2007-08 to open 2013-14 EP sub-concession.	2 000 of which 1 000 are under construction, of which 430 are highways that could be tolled.	EP makes availability payments to private partner and receives tolls collected by the private partner.	Only 240 km of the new highways are tolled.	Demand risk.

Source: Estradas de Portugal.

The large PPP programme has created a significant and growing payment obligation for the government (Figure 1.10). The PPP payment obligations have a net present value of EUR 10.7 billion (6.3% of GDP) in 2012 and yearly payments are projected to rise from EUR 1 billion in 2012 to EUR 1.5 billion by 2015 as new roads currently under construction are completed. The payment problem has become more acute with the sovereign debt crisis as EP can no longer access market finance (despite being operationally profitable) and is therefore fully reliant on financing from the central government.

Significant risk surrounds these net payment projections. Net payments by the government were 20% higher than forecast in both 2011 and 2010 albeit essentially due to one-off factors. The largest risks lie in transport PPPs (road and rail) arising from assumptions such as traffic flows (DGTF, 2011b). Indeed, there are some signs that toll revenue projections could prove too optimistic. Although this is difficult to separate from recessionary effects, demand appears to have reacted strongly to the introduction of real tolls on former shadow toll roads, with traffic declining by half on one of them. The allocation of risk between public and private parties is complex and depends on the particular PPP. In general, for road design, building and maintenance, availability and raising finance risk usually lie with the private sector as well as demand for private concessions for real toll roads (DGTF, 2011b).

Figure 1.10. **Net public-private partnership payments by the government**
Per cent of GDP

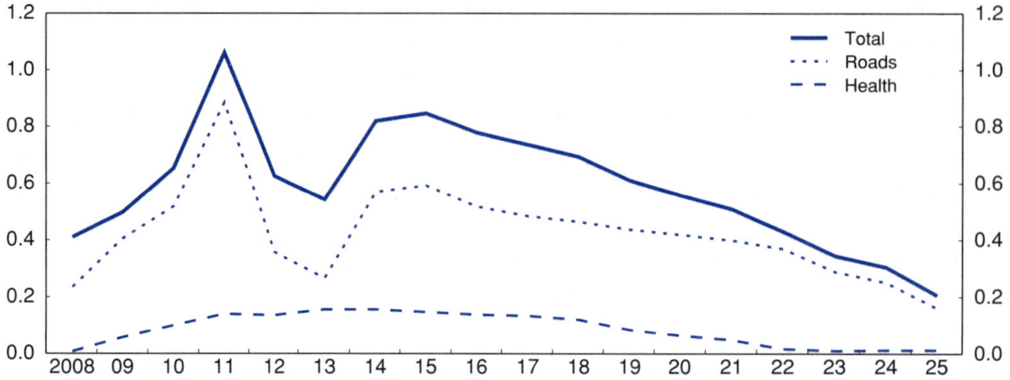

Source: DGTF (2010), "Public Private Partnerships and Concessions 2010 Report" and DGTF (2011), *Boletim Informativo Parcerias Público-Privadas e Concessões* 4.º Trimestre 2011, Direcção – Geral do Tesouro e Finanças; and Ministry of Finance (2011), *Orçamento do Estado para 2012, Relatório.*

StatLink ⟶ http://dx.doi.org/10.1787/888932669876

The government carries demand risk in the case of EP sub-concessions where the government receives toll revenue from users, which are now the dominant concession model. In addition, under contracts signed prior to 2003 the government carried the risk of extra costs of having to relocate to different land for a road corridor, for example due to environmental reasons, which was part of the reason PPP payments exceeded forecasts in both 2010 and 2011. Generally the government should only transfer risks to the private sector that the private sector can control such as construction risk (Araújo and Sutherland, 2010). In the case of roads it is arguable that the private partner can influence demand, for example through road quality, and therefore should bear at least some of this risk rather than transferring all of it to the government as has been done with the EP concessions.

As part of the programme, no new PPP contract will be signed in the short term and the pressing policy issue is to reduce future costs and risks arising from existing PPPs. The government has already taken action to start reducing its obligations. In the rail area, the three high speed train (TGV) projects (Lisbon-Porto and Porto-Vigo and the link to Spain) have been cancelled. In the roads area, the conversion of former shadow toll roads to toll roads is a welcome addition to revenue for these projects and the government should extend coverage to the approximately 200 kilometres of highway that is currently not designated for tolls yet. The government has also engaged an international accounting firm to report in June in more detail the contingent liabilities under the PPPs and the probability of these materialising. It also assessed the costs and benefits of further renegotiation of the PPP contracts. To resolve existing PPPs, a mixture of measures could be taken, depending on the exact circumstances of each PPP including: renegotiating terms; cancelling projects when still at an early stage; or the buying back of PPP roads (Reis, 2012).

In the future, PPPs can still potentially be a useful model for delivery services, particularly when there is a positive externality between the construction and operating phases, which gives incentives for the private sector to internalise the costs of service provision and asset maintenance in its decisions at the construction phase (Araújo and Sutherland, 2010). However, they should be chosen because they represent good value for money and not to postpone expenditure. The literature and international experience suggest a number of factors that can help to ensure that a PPP is the right delivery model and maximises value for money.

These include specifying contracts in terms of outputs instead of inputs in order to maximise the benefits of private sector technical expertise and management skills; an *ex ante* evaluation of PPP versus public procurement; a public body obtaining planning and environmental permissions in advance of tender to avoid delays; and proper fiscal accounting for PPPs including recording them in contingent liabilities (Araújo and Sutherland, 2010).

By international standards, the efficiency enhancing features of Portugal's PPP framework appear relatively strong on paper and the government is intending further improvements (Figure 1.11). It is setting up a technical unit of around ten PPP experts in the Ministry of Finance to advise the minister on all aspects of launching, designing and monitoring PPP projects where investment exceeds EUR 25 million. This is welcome, as expertise is a key constraint on getting the most out of the PPP model. Similar units exist in Ireland and Italy. Such a unit can also have useful role in spreading knowledge to local government, which has less experience in managing PPPs.

Figure 1.11. **Indicator of efficiency constraining features of public-private partnership frameworks**
Index scale of 0-6 from least to most restrictive, 2008

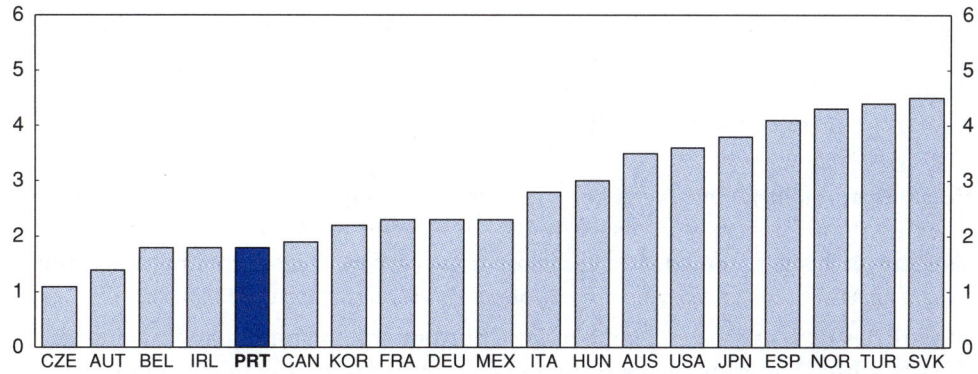

Source: S. Araújo and D. Sutherland (2010), "Public-Private Partnerships and Investment in Infrastructure", *OECD Economics Department Working Papers*, No. 803.

StatLink ⟶ http://dx.doi.org/10.1787/888932669895

However, past experience shows that it is important that the new framework is actually implemented and in particular that analysis done by the unit is fully taken into account by political decisions. In this regard, the government's intention that all PPP project proposals will be compared against an ordinary public procurement alternative and the results made publicly available and presented to the parliament is welcome. In addition, there is a need for a proper assessment of the full implications for the budget position of PPPs over their whole life-cycle and the government should further reform how PPPs are included in the budget planning by accounting for capital expenditure on them on the same basis as the alternative of an ordinary public investment.

Local and regional governments' debt issues are leading the central government to step in

Portugal is a fairly centralised country (Box 1.1), but subnational government nevertheless poses important fiscal issues. Since 2009, local and regional authorities have faced declining revenues, due to cuts in central government transfers and depressed tax receipts, particularly on housing transactions. They reacted by cutting spending, but not rapidly enough to prevent the accumulation of debt (Figure 1.12). The total deficit of local government (including autonomous regions) reached 0.8% of GDP in 2009-10, before halving in 2011. Local debt has risen to a high international level (Figure 1.13) and local governments have lost access to long-term bank credit in the wake of the sovereign debt crisis. As a result, a large number of municipalities as well as the region of Madeira have accumulated unsustainable short-term debt and payment arrears, notably through local public companies. This makes it difficult to assess the total extent of their liabilities, although audits carried out by the central government in the first half of 2012 resulted in significant progress in this direction.

> **Box 1.1. The structure of Portuguese subnational government**
>
> There are no elected regional governments on the mainland, meaning that local government is essentially concentrated at the municipal level and in the two autonomous regions of the Azores and Madeira. Municipalities are relatively large by European standards (34 000 inhabitants on average) and are subdivided into civil parishes in charge of lower administrative functions. More precisely, Portugal is subdivided into:
>
> - **2 autonomous regions:** the Azores and Madeira, which enjoy a large autonomy guaranteed by the Portuguese Constitution, elect their own regional government and legislative assembly and keep tax receipts collected in their jurisdiction. In addition, the mainland is subdivided in five regions, which were originally created to manage EU structural funds, and whose role has grown to include wider regional development issues. Mainland regions have no elected government and are directly administered by central government representatives – the so-called Commissions for Regional Coordination and Development (CCDR).
>
> - **308 municipalities** – mainly in charge of basic infrastructure and primary education. They are run by an executive council and a municipal assembly, both elected for four years. In the past few years, municipalities have been encouraged to associate into inter-municipal communities, which have the right to collect certain taxes and have a bigger role in the management of EU funds.
>
> - **4 259 civil parishes** (*freguesias*) – in charge of local current administration and maintenance of certain basic infrastructure. The number of parishes per municipalities (14 on average) varies widely, from 1 to 89. Parishes are managed by a local assembly and an elected local council, the president of which also sits in the municipal assembly. Their economic weight is relatively small, with an overall budget of around EUR 450 million (0.3% of GDP).

Figure 1.12. **Local government revenue and expenditure**[1]

Per cent growth

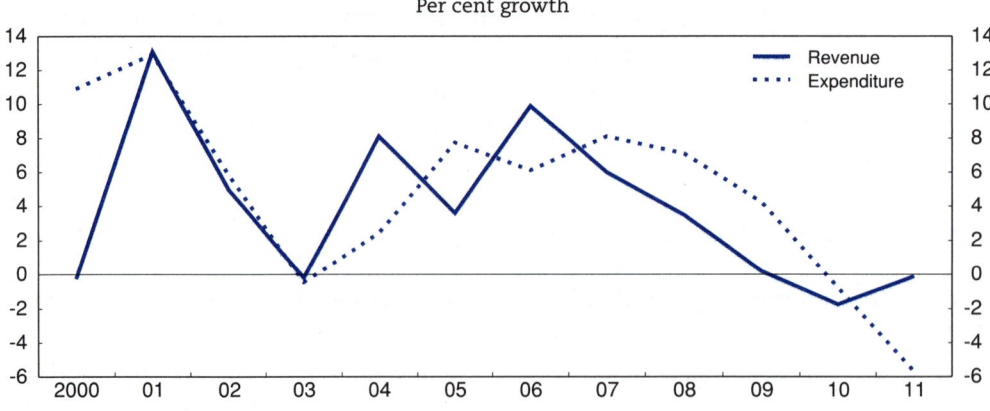

1. Includes autonomous regions.
Source: OECD (2012), "General Government Accounts", *OECD National Accounts Statistics* (database), May.
StatLink http://dx.doi.org/10.1787/888932669914

Figure 1.13. **Local government debt**[1]
Per cent of local government revenue

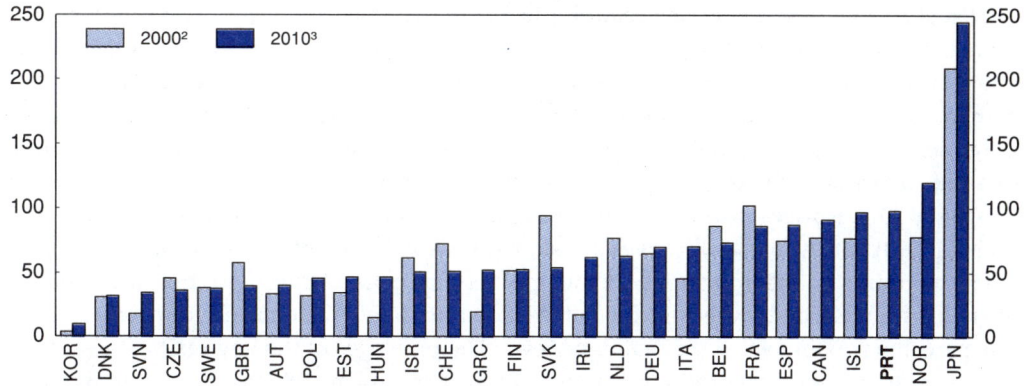

1. Total liabilities of subnational authorities excluding insurance technical reserves. Non-consolidated debt except for Israel.
2. 2001 for Israel and Slovenia, 2002 for Korea.
3. 2009 for Korea and Switzerland.
Source: OECD (2012), *OECD National Accounts Statistics* (database), June.

StatLink http://dx.doi.org/10.1787/888932669933

Supporting local governments involves a trade-off

Faced with severe fiscal problems in the autonomous region of Madeira, the central government decided to step in with a EUR 1.5 billion (0.9% of GDP) financial assistance plan (Box 1.2). The government also agreed to support distressed municipalities with a EUR 1 billion (0.6% of GDP) credit line. This will allow municipalities to pay back part of their short-term debt and arrears, the total of which for all local and regional authorities reached EUR 4 billion (2.3% of GDP) by the end of 2011.[2] In exchange for this support, municipalities have notably committed to cut spending and increase taxes (where possible) and fees. The government expects more than half of municipalities to apply for the credit line. Applications will be examined by the government in mid-2012. In this context, it is important that the conditions under which municipalities receive support, and how much support each municipality is entitled to, follow strict and transparent guidelines, as envisaged, to ensure equal treatment of municipalities and avoid political interference.

> **Box 1.2. The financial assistance plan to Madeira**
>
> Once Portugal's poorest region, Madeira has become the country's second richest over recent decades, thanks notably to large subsidies from the central government and the EU. In 2008, regional GDP per capita was 30% higher than the national average. Large infrastructure works have helped develop tourism – the island's main activity (20% of regional GDP) – while a low-tax business zone has attracted important off-shore business activities (20% of regional GDP). Over the past few years, subsidies have become less abundant as a result of the region's economic progress. However, public spending has not slowed accordingly, leading to the rapid accumulation of debts as large construction projects were still undertaken, including a marina and a heliport (both of which are out-of-use because of flawed design).

> **Box 1.2. The financial assistance plan to Madeira** *(cont.)*
>
> Unsustainable debt dynamics resulted in Madeira's regional government looking for financial support. The central government agreed in January 2012 to provide EUR 1.5 billion (0.9% of national GDP, 30% of regional GDP) of loans to the region, with an interest rate comparable to the central government's financing costs. The fiscal consolidation plan aimed at reducing the regional public deficit from 6% of regional GDP in 2011 (excluding negative one-offs of 11% of regional GDP) to 3% of regional GDP in 2012, 1% in 2013 and to balance the budget by 2014. However, the 2011 deficit turned out higher than expected by 3½ per cent of regional GDP, putting these objectives at risk. The consolidation relies mainly on the revenue side (two thirds of the adjustment).* Income tax and general corporate tax rates will be aligned with mainland levels and the value-added tax rate will be raised from 16% to 21%, one percentage point below the mainland level. The privileges of the low-tax business zone will be reduced, with a corporate tax rate raised from 0% to 4%. On the spending side, measures include a cap on public investment at EUR 150 million per year – roughly its underlying level in 2010-11 after correcting for one-offs – and lower public wages, mainly as a result of the national level cut in the 13th and 14th month of civil servants' salary.
>
> Financial assistance is conditional on a strong reinforcement of the fiscal framework. The budget will be subject to central government approval before it is voted and its execution will be closely monitored. An audit on arrears, which amount to 40% of regional GDP has been carried out in early 2012. However, the size of the region's total liabilities, *i.e.* including all liabilities of local public companies, is still uncertain. These companies are planned to be restructured and partly privatised. No new public-private partnership (PPP) can be contracted until existing PPPs are audited and renegotiated. Disbursements of the central government loans will be spread over 2012-15 and conditional to the region complying with the programme. Compliance will be assessed through quarterly mission reviews, starting in April 2012. Such a strict conditionality is important, as the constitutional autonomy of the region otherwise restricts the central government's ability to influence the region's policy, as illustrated by its inability in 2011 to stop construction projects judged too costly.
>
> * However, against a no-policy change scenario, the programme contains more measures on the spending side than on the revenue side, reflecting that a large planned increase in public investment in 2012 (EUR 400 million, excluding one-offs) was cancelled as part of the programme, meaning that public investment will remain broadly stable between 2011 and 2012 (excluding one-offs).

The central government does not explicitly guarantee local debts and faces a trade-off between supporting distressed local authorities and letting them default. On the one hand, financial support to local governments could generate significant fiscal costs for the central government at a time of scarce fiscal resources. These costs would also risk increasing in the future if the economic outlook (and thus local revenues) deteriorates further. Another drawback is moral hazard, as the possibility of financial assistance could undermine prudence in future local policymaking, as occurred in Sweden in the 1970s-80s (Pettersson-Lidbom and Dahlberg, 2003). On the other hand, a wave of local defaults would impose losses on Portuguese banks, thus augmenting already significant recapitalisation needs. In the current context, it could also affect investors' confidence in other public borrowers, including the central government itself. Overall, this suggests that financial assistance should be provided to distressed local government in cases of liquidity problems, *i.e.* when limited and temporary support would suffice to restore debt sustainability, but that the government should be ready to accept defaults of insolvent authorities in some instances, so as to reduce moral hazard issues.

In the case of Madeira, there are significant risks to the programme as the 2011 deficit turned out higher than expected and the region's total liabilities (including arrears and debt from local public companies) are still unknown, but may be as high as 150% of regional GDP. In addition, the programme assumption that the region will grow at the same pace as the country as a whole appears to be relatively fragile, especially given the traditionally high reliance on public demand in the region. The programme's success will depend on the region's capacity to find new sources of private growth despite the increase in taxes and to respect expenditure targets, notably on public investment. This will require a strong reinforcement of the regional fiscal framework. The central government should carefully monitor the solvency of the region as there is a significant risk that the region may not be able to pay back all of its debt, thereby making debt restructuring inevitable.

Measures are needed to improve the local and regional fiscal framework

It is also important that financial support to municipalities be accompanied by an enhanced local and regional fiscal framework to ensure debt reduction in the medium-term. To this end, the government is committed to presenting revised local and regional financing laws by the end of 2012. Important steps in this area were already taken in the 2007 reform of the local finance law, which notably requires municipalities to consolidate their accounts with those of local public companies and to submit them to external auditing. However, implementation of these measures has been delayed by municipal opposition (Blöchliger and Vammalle, 2012). In the current context, implementing them rapidly should be a priority. The 2007 reform also introduced limits on municipal total debt (125% of annual revenues) and short-term debt (10% of annual revenues). In order to prevent any circumventing of these rules, their scope should be broadened to include all liabilities of local authorities, such as payment arrears, debts of local public companies and discounted future payments in PPP contracts. Additionally, a balanced budget rule could be introduced, a relatively common feature across OECD local governments (Sutherland et al., 2005) that would offer the benefit of consistency with the general government's broader deficit rule.

The local fiscal framework should also give incentives for local and regional authorities to pay back arrears, which had accumulated to almost EUR 2.8 billion (1.6% of GDP) by the end of 2011 and were still increasing in the first months of 2012. To this end, the government intends to apply to municipalities the budgetary "commitment control" framework which has been put in place at the central level. In this framework, entities are not allowed to spend more money than they project to receive and entities with spending arrears are forced to adopt more ambitious spending limits. To make the framework fully efficient, it will be necessary to prevent municipalities from relying on over-optimistic revenue forecasts, a frequent practice in the past. This will require giving the Ministry of Finance a supervisory role in this area, while the Fiscal Council could also be involved in monitoring tasks. In addition, municipalities should be required to keep their funds in a dedicated account at the Treasury (instead of a private bank account), as a way to facilitate monitoring and to reduce general government gross public debt (via more debt consolidation).

The cyclicality of local revenues should be reduced

Local revenues are particularly cyclical and their abrupt decline in the last few years has been an important factor behind the accumulation of local debt. Local revenues include a housing transaction tax and a corporate tax, both of which are by nature very sensitive to the economic cycle (Box 1.3). For example, transaction tax revenues have declined by 40% between 2007 and 2009 (Figure 1.14). Moreover, transfers from the central government also decline in economic downturns. This revenue volatility is problematic because local governments are generally less well-equipped to cope with revenue swings than central governments (Norregaard, 1997). In the eventuality a balanced budget rule for local authorities was introduced, reducing this volatility would be even more important as local governments would otherwise be forced into a very pro-cyclical spending behaviour.

> Box 1.3. **Municipalities have cyclical resources and little fiscal autonomy**
>
> Municipalities draw roughly half of their resources from local taxes and fees and the other half from transfers from the central government and from EU structural funds. The poorest municipalities tend to be more dependent on transfers as they have lower tax revenues. Local taxes are mainly housing related, concerning both property (30% of local tax revenues) and transactions (20% of local tax revenues). Municipalities set rates for the former, within a centrally defined range, but not for the latter. Other tax resources include a local corporate income tax (*derrama*) and a fraction of the vehicle tax. Municipalities' relatively low fiscal autonomy was slightly increased in 2007, by allowing them to claim up to 5% of their residents' personal income tax, the principle being that unclaimed receipts remain with taxpayers.
>
> Concerning transfers from the central government, municipalities receive a quarter of personal income tax, corporate income tax and value-added tax national revenues. These revenues are distributed on the basis of demographic, geographic and environmental criteria with an equalisation scheme ensuring strong redistribution towards the poorest municipalities. There is no mechanism to smooth these transfers, meaning that a fall in national tax revenues is directly translated into falling transfers to municipalities, albeit with a two year lag. Transfers from the central government to municipalities also include earmarked funds to finance specific spending on education, health and social policy.

Figure 1.14. **Local government tax revenue in Portugal**
Million euros

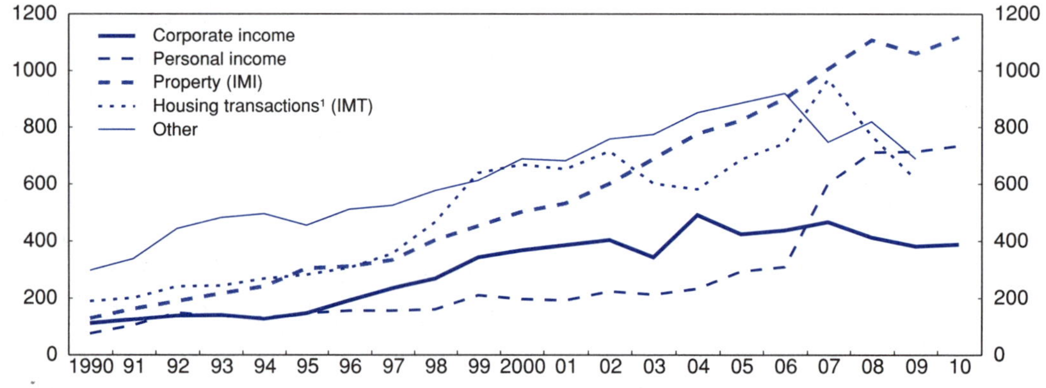

1. Since 1995 this tax is collected by central government but then transferred to local government.
Source: OECD (2012), "Revenue Statistics: Portugal", *OECD Tax Statistics* (database), May.
StatLink ⟶ http://dx.doi.org/10.1787/888932669952

Several measures would help to reduce the cyclicality of local revenues. Firstly, housing taxation should be shifted from transactions to recurrent taxation of immovable property, as recommended in the 2010 *Survey*. Such a measure would make local revenues less volatile but also foster labour mobility, thus stimulating potential growth. Secondly, transfers from central to local governments should be set in advance on a multi-year basis. This would reduce their volatility and give municipalities more certainty about their future resources, which would represent a fair counterpart to stricter monitoring being imposed by the central government. Another benefit of this would be that it would limit the scope for higher transfers to local governments in election years, as there is evidence that, despite the existing rules, electoral motives currently lead to such a bias (Veiga and Veiga, 2011). A third option would be to increase local authorities' fiscal autonomy, which is low by international standards, to enable them to cope with revenue declines by increasing local taxes. This could also lead to more efficient public service by increasing local government's accountability to taxpayers (Blöchliger and Pinero-Campos, 2011; Joumard and Kongsrud, 2003). However, this option should only be considered once local efforts to rationalise spending have been completed as the prospect of additional tax resources may undermine these efforts. Finally, a common practice is that municipalities levy "compensations" from businesses (*e.g.* wind turbine farms, retailers) establishing in their jurisdiction. This possibility should be reduced to make municipalities less dependent on this uncertain revenue source, which is also harmful for the business environment.

There is large scope to make local spending more efficient

Enhancing the efficiency of local spending will be crucial to achieving successful consolidation as heavy spending cuts are needed to balance local budgets in a context of declining revenues. Empirical work suggests that there is large scope for efficiency gains, as high as 40% on the sample of municipalities constituted by the Lisbon region (Afonso and Fernandes, 2003). Indeed, municipalities have had few incentives for efficiency over the past decade as a result of dynamic revenue growth, cheap credit and a weak fiscal framework, notably in terms of local public companies, which has allowed them to pile up debts. Excessive fragmentation is also a source of inefficiencies, with certain parishes containing only a few hundred people and inter-municipal cooperation still nascent. Rigidities in terms of labour contracts, which are required to be similar to central government contracts, may also have limited municipalities' flexibility in terms of staffing. However, this feature will now probably help reduce local spending as the central government is implementing large cuts in public wages. Finally, local governments have a tendency to invest excessively in infrastructure, despite basic needs in this area being already largely satisfied (da Silva, 2008, Chapter 2), which suggests that in the eventuality a local balanced budget rule is introduced, it should include capital expenditures.

To improve spending efficiency, the authorities are committed to presenting new laws, before the end of 2012, concerning both municipalities and autonomous regions. Measures will include an assessment and a restructuring of local public companies, a 30% cut in the number of parishes (with a stronger focus on urban areas) and a facilitation of inter-municipal cooperation (Portuguese Government, 2011). These welcome measures should be complemented by the generalisation of benchmarking and performance indicators, which can be powerful tools to foster local spending efficiency (Mizell, 2006; OECD, 2009d) as illustrated *e.g.* by the success of the "Kostra" system in Norway (OECD,

2008b, Box 3.11). In this area, first efforts could concentrate on the domains of water, wastewater and waste management, where indicators would facilitate efforts to streamline the local public corporate sector, while also bringing environmental benefits (OECD, 2011b). In addition, a purchasing cooperative could be created to take advantage of economies of scale when purchasing supplies.

Making better use of EU structural funds would mitigate fiscal consolidation

EU structural and cohesion funds are a significant resource for the Portuguese economy, amounting to around 2% of GDP per year (Box 1.4). Spending them efficiently is now all the more important that they are one of the few remaining sources of financing for the economy in the current context of deleveraging and fiscal consolidation. The first challenge is to ensure that all available funds are spent despite the serious financing constraints faced by national partners, which have notably led to the cancellation of large infrastructure projects (new Lisbon airport, high-speed Lisbon-Madrid train). The second and most important challenge is to put funds to their most productive use. This notably implies reinforcing governance to prevent efforts to absorb funds from undermining careful project selection and to reduce scope for political interference as there is empirical evidence of electoral motivations influencing funds' allocation to municipalities (Veiga, 2010).

> **Box 1.4. EU structural and cohesion funds in Portugal**
>
> Portugal is the biggest recipient of EU structural and cohesion funds among "old" EU member States, with an allocation of 1.8% of GDP per year for 2007-13 (Figure 1.15). Funds allocated to Portugal are split roughly evenly between three priorities: "territorial enhancement" (mainly infrastructure investment), "competitiveness" (support to companies and innovation) and "human potential" (education and training, including school infrastructures). When compared with past programmes and other countries, this implies more focus on education and less on infrastructure, reflecting that Portuguese basic infrastructure needs are now broadly satisfied while the lack of education remains an important bottleneck to growth.
>
> **Figure 1.15. Absorption of EU structural and cohesion funds by end 2011**
> Funds allocated over 2007-13
>
>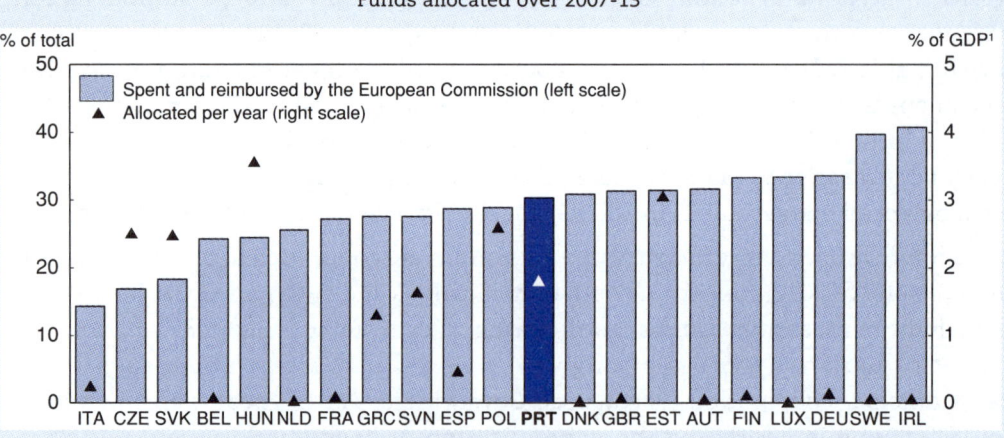
>
> 1. Average for the period 2007-13, Eurostat projections.
> Source: QREN (2012), "Indicadores Conjunturais de Monitorização", Boletim Informativo 14, Comissão Técnica de Coordenação do Qren and Eurostat (2012), "Economy and Finance", Eurostat Database, May.
> StatLink ⟶ http://dx.doi.org/10.1787/888932669971

> **Box 1.4. EU structural and cohesion funds in Portugal** *(cont.)*
>
> The selection of projects financed by EU funds is carried out by national and regional authorities within a framework of operational programmes reflecting the three national priorities. Each programme can receive financing from one or several of the three EU funds: the European Regional Development Fund for activities such as infrastructure investment and support to small and medium-sized enterprises, the European Social Fund mostly for education, and the Cohesion Fund for transport and environment related activities. In Portugal, private projects are chosen by selection committees after public calls for projects, while public projects are either directly integrated into public policy programmes (*e.g.* school building programmes) or selected by national authorities in accordance with publicly disclosed guidelines agreed upon with local stakeholders. Large infrastructure projects (exceeding EUR 50 million) also require *ex ante* cost-benefit analyses and explicit approval by the European Commission. Monitoring is mainly a national responsibility, with the European Commission only in charge of monitoring national governance frameworks and dedicating relatively low means to combat fraud.*
>
> * Financial Times (2010), "Net That Fails to Catch EUR 700m Errors", In-depth Report on EU Structural Funds, 30 November.

In terms of the absorption of EU funds, Portugal is doing better than in the preceding cycle (Marzinetto, 2011) and than most other big recipients of funds (Figure 1.15). By the end of 2011, 80% of the funds allocated for 2007-13 – which have to be spent no later than 2015 – had already been committed to selected projects, 40% had been effectively spent and 30% had already been reimbursed by the European Commission (Portuguese Government, 2012). To stimulate absorption, the Portuguese authorities are progressively shifting money from transport and environment infrastructure programmes, where many projects have been cancelled, to other programmes, notably related to education. To this end, an assessment of inactive projects was carried out in April 2012, aiming to free up to EUR 1.5 billion of funds for reallocation. The absorption of funds will also be increased by the EU decision in December 2011 to reduce local co-financing rates in crisis countries, which, for Portugal, could bring it from an average 30% down to 15%. This lower co-financing will apply for 2010-13, but only retroactively, *i.e.* on projects already selected, to avoid attracting lower quality projects.

In this context, available EU funds should be strategically shifted towards two of Portugal's most pressing economic priorities: alleviating the credit squeeze on small and medium-sized enterprises (SME) and avoiding high unemployment becoming structural. Regarding the former, additional resources should be devolved to provide financing or guarantees to viable SMEs, which may require further approval by the European Commission to reallocate funds across programmes. In addition, measures should be taken to facilitate SMEs' participation in EU funded projects, *e.g.* by clarifying tender processes, providing SMEs with support to comply with (cumbersome) administrative procedures and giving SMEs more say about the strategic allocation of funds. To tackle the unemployment problem better, funds should be further shifted towards active labour market policies such as targeted training programmes for (especially young) unemployed, a move also encouraged by the European authorities (European Council, 2012).

In addition, further efforts are needed to improve governance, especially in a context of lower co-financing rates. At the macro level, a ministerial coordination committee, chaired by the Finance Minister, has recently been created. It may help address the need for high-level arbitration in the strategic allocation of funds both across sectors and across regions (Barca *et al.*, 2012). A strategic monitoring process is also being introduced to assess the efficiency of policies and reorient funds if needed. This is welcome as continuous evaluation and benchmarking are essential to make an efficient use of funds (OECD, 2009d). Such evaluation should be generalised, carried out by an independent body and its results should be published. At a more micro level, there is also scope to rationalise the allocation of funds by generalising *ex ante* economic analyses and by delegating the selection of public projects to more independent and more accountable agencies in order to reduce political interference. In addition, more means should be dedicated to combat fraud as "soft" investment projects such as training programmes tend to be more difficult to monitor than infrastructure projects. Finally, more dialogue should be encouraged at the regional level between central government representatives and local stakeholders in order to stimulate the emergence of bottom-up projects taking better into account regional interests (OECD, 2008b).

> **Box 1.5. Summary of recommendations for restoring fiscal sustainability and lifting public sector efficiency**
>
> **Fiscal policy and fiscal framework**
>
> - The government should aim to meet headline deficit targets in the programme, notably through abiding by the budgeted expenditure at all levels of general government. If risks materialise significantly and growth is far lower than projected in the programme, the automatic stabilisers could be allowed to operate at least partially.
> - Introduce an explicit and easily enforceable public expenditure rule consistent with revenue projections and medium-term fiscal objectives and in line with the European fiscal framework.
> - The Fiscal Council should prioritise core functions, including assessing the macroeconomic and fiscal projections, compliance with fiscal rules and giving fiscal policy recommendations to the government. Fiscal council board members should be allowed to have other paid employment.
> - The Minister of Finance should be required to provide a formal response to fiscal council reports to embed the fiscal council's role in the policy debate.
>
> **State-owned enterprises and public-private partnerships**
>
> - To improve transparency around state-owned enterprises (SOE), explicitly set and show in the government's accounts the subsidy paid to urban transport companies in return for an agreed level of services and at least operational balance.
> - Continue to rationalise the rail network and services replacing less frequented lines with bus services to improve SOE performance.
> - Future public-private partnerships (PPP) should be budgeted for in the same way as other investment to avoid PPPs being used as a way to push expenditure into the future.
>
> **Local government and EU structural funds**
>
> - As envisaged, support to local and regional governments should come only under strict and transparent guidelines and be accompanied by improvements in the fiscal framework. Municipalities should notably be required to keep their funds in a dedicated account at the Treasury.
> - Local government revenues should be made less volatile by shifting from taxing housing transactions to higher recurrent taxation of immovable property and by setting government transfers on a multi-year basis.
> - Local spending efficiency should be encouraged by the generalisation of benchmarking and performance indicators.
> - Absorption of EU structural funds should be further stimulated by shifting available funds towards credit to SMEs and targeted training programmes, while governance should be reinforced to enhance efficiency.

Notes

1. More exactly, assuming a constant elasticity of revenue to GDP:

$$\Delta sb_t = \left(\frac{\frac{EXP_{t-1}}{GDP_{t-1}} + \frac{EXP_t}{GDP_t}}{2} \right) \times (\alpha_t - g_t) \times \frac{1}{1 + (\alpha_t - (g_t - \alpha_t)/2)}$$

where Δsb is the change in the structural balance, EXP is expenditure, GDP is nominal potential GDP, g is the growth rate of nominal potential GDP and α is the growth rate of total expenditure.

2. Combined arrears of local and regional governments reached EUR 2.8 billion by the end of 2011 (European Commission, 2012), while their short term debt (less than one year) was EUR 1.3 billion (Bank of Portugal, 2012).

Bibliography

Afonso, A. and S. Fernandes (2003), "Efficiency of Local Government Spending: Evidence for the Lisbon Region", *Working Papers*, No. 2003/09, Department of Economics at the School of Economics and Management (ISEG), Technical University of Lisbon.

Ahrend, R., J. Arnold and C. Moeser (2011), "The Sharing of Macroeconomic Risk", *OECD Economics Department Working Papers*, No. 877, OECD Publishing.

Araújo, S. and D. Sutherland (2010), "Public-Private Partnerships and Investment in Infrastructure", *OECD Economics Department Working Papers*, No. 803, OECD Publishing.

Arnold, J. (2008), "Do Tax Structures Affect Aggregate Economic Growth?: Empirical Evidence from a Panel of OECD Countries", *OECD Economics Department Working Papers*, No. 643, OECD Publishing.

Bank of Portugal (2012), *Statistical Bulletin*, May.

Barca, F., P. McCann and A. Rodríguez-Pose (2012), "The Case for Regional Development Intervention: Place-Based Versus Place-Neutral Approaches", *Journal of Regional Science*, Vol. 52, No. 1.

Blöchliger, H. and C. Vammalle (2012), "Portugal: the Reform of the Local Finance Law", *Reforming Fiscal Federalism and Local Government: Beyond the Zero-Sum Game*, OECD Fiscal Federalism Studies, OECD Publishing.

Blöchliger, H. and J.M. Pinero-Campos (2011), "Tax Competition between Sub-Central Governments", *OECD Economics Department Working Papers*, No. 872, OECD Publishing.

Brzozowski, M. and J. Siwinska-Gorzelak (2010), "The Impact of Fiscal Rules on Fiscal Policy Volatility", *Journal of Applied Economics*, Vol. 13, No. 2, Elsevier.

Callan, T., C. Leventi, H. Levy, M. Matsaganis, A. Paulus and H. Sutherland (2011), "The Distributional Effects of Austerity Measures: A Comparison of Six Countries", *Research Note*, No. 2, Social Situation Observatory, European Commission.

Calmfors, L. (2010), "The Swedish Fiscal Policy Council – Experiences and Lessons", paper presented at the Conference on Independent Fiscal Policy Institutions, 18-19 March, Budapest.

Calmfors, L. and S. Wren-Lewis (2011), "What Should Fiscal Councils Do?", *Economic Policy*, Vol. 26, No. 68, Blackwell Publishing.

Celasun, O., X. Debrun and J.D. Ostry (2006), "Primary Surplus Behaviour and Risks to Fiscal Sustainability in Emerging Market Countries: A 'Fan-Chart' Approach", *IMF Working Paper*, No. 06/67, International Monetary Fund.

Corsetti, G., A. Meier, G. Müller (2012), "What Determines Government Spending Multipliers?", *IMF Working Paper*, No. 12/150, International Monetary Fund.

Debrun, X., D. Hauner and M.S. Kumar (2009), "Independent Fiscal Agencies", *Journal of Economic Surveys*, Vol. 23, No. 1, Wiley Blackwell.

DGTF (Direcção-Geral do Tresouro e Finanças) (2011a), *Sector Empresarial do Estado Relatório 2011*.

DGTF (2011b), *Parcerias Público-Privadas e Concessões Relatório 2011*, Direcção-Geral do Tesouro e Finanças.

EPEC (European PPP Expertise Centre) (2010) "Market Update: Review of the European PPP Market in 2010".

European Commission (2012), "The Economic Adjustment Programme for Portugal, Third Review", *Occasional Paper*, No. 95, April.

European Council (2011), "Statement by the Euro Area Heads of State or Government", Brussels, 9 December.

European Council (2012), "Statement of the Members of the European Council, 31 January 2012".

Guichard, S., M. Kennedy, E. Wurzel and C. André (2007), "What Promotes Fiscal Consolidation: OECD Country Experiences", *OECD Economics Department Working Papers*, No. 553, OECD Publishing.

Hagemann, R. (2010), "Improving Fiscal Performance Through Fiscal Councils", *OECD Economics Department Working Papers*, No. 829, OECD Publishing.

Hauptmeier, S.A., J. Sanchez-Fuentes and L. Schuknecht (2011), "Towards Expenditure Rules and Fiscal Sanity in the Euro Area", *Journal of Policy Modeling*, Vol. 33, No. 4, Elsevier.

Intrum Justitia (2011), *European Payment Index 2011*, Intrum Justitia AB.

IMF (International Monetary Fund) (2009), *Fiscal Rules – Anchoring Expectations for Sustainable Public Finances*.

Joumard, I. and P. Kongsrud (2003), "Fiscal Relations Across Government Levels", *OECD Economic Studies*, No. 36, OECD Publishing.

Kappeler, A. and M. Nemoz (2010), "Public-Private Partnerships in Europe – Before and During the Recent Financial Crisis", *Economic and Financial Report*, No. 4, European Investment Bank.

Kopits, G. (2011), "Independent Fiscal Institutions: Developing Good Practices", *OECD Journal on Budgeting*, Vol. 11, No. 3, OECD Publishing.

Lenain, P., R. Hagemann and D. Carey (2010), "Restoring Fiscal Sustainability in the United States", *OECD Economics Department Working Papers*, No. 806, OECD Publishing.

Marzinetto, B. (2011), "A European Fund for Economic Revival in Crisis Countries", *Bruegel Policy Contributions*, No. 2011/01, Bruegel.

Minstry of Economy (2011), *Plano Estratégico dos Transportes, Mobilidade Sustentável, Horizonte, 2011-15*, Ministéro da Economia e do Emprego, October.

Ministry of Finance (2011a), "Fiscal Strategy Document 2011-2015", Ministério das Finanças, August.

Ministry of Finance (2011b), "Note on the Portuguese Fiscal Consolidation 2010 and 2011", *Press Release*, 5 April, Ministério das Finanças.

Mizell, L. (2006), "Promoting Performance: Using Indicators to Enhance the Effectiveness of Sub Central Spending", *Fiscal Federalism Network Working Papers*, No. 5, OECD Publishing.

Norregaard, J. (1997), "Tax Assignment", *Fiscal Federalism in Theory and Practice*, T. Ter-Minasian (ed.), International Monetary Fund.

OECD (2002), "OECD Best Practices for Budget Transparency", *OECD Journal on Budgeting*, Vol. 1, No. 3, OECD Publishing.

OECD (2008a), *OECD Review of Budgeting in Portugal*, OECD Publishing.

OECD (2008b), *OECD Territorial Reviews: Portugal 2008*, OECD Publishing.

OECD (2009a), *OECD Economic Outlook, Interim Report March 2009*, OECD Publishing.

OECD (2009b), *Government at a Glance 2009*, OECD Publishing.

OECD (2009c), *OECD Economic Surveys: United Kingdom 2009*, OECD Publishing.

OECD (2009d), *Governing Regional Development Policy: The Use of Performance Indicators*, OECD Publishing.

OECD (2011a), "Budgeting Features that Strengthen Fiscal Policy in OECD Countries: Results from the OECD Budget Practices and Procedures Database", GOV/PGC/SBO(2011)11, paper presented at the 7th Annual Meeting of OECD Senior Budget Officials Network on Performance and Results, 9-10 November.

OECD (2011b), *Environmental Performance Reviews: Portugal 2011*, OECD Publishing.

Pettersson-Lidbom, P. and M. Dahlberg, (2003), "An Empirical Approach for Evaluating Soft Budget Constraints", *Working Paper Series*, No. 28, Department of Economics, Uppsala University.

Portuguese Government (2011), "Documento Verde da Reforma da Administração Local", Gabinete do Ministro Adjunto e dos Assuntos Parlamentares.

Portuguese Government (2012), "Indicadores Conjunturais de Monitoração", *Boletim Informativo*, No. 14, Comissão Técnica de Coordenação do QREN.

Portuguese Public Finance Council (2012), "Portugal's Fiscal Strategy 2012-2016", *Report*, No. 1/2012, Conselho das Finanças Públicas.

Reis, R.F. (2012), "The Impact of PPPs Contracting on Portugal's Fiscal Position and What Can Be Done About It", Presentation at the 5th annual OECD meeting on Public-Private Partnerships, March.

Schick, A. (2010), "Post Crisis Fiscal Rules: Stabilising Public Finance while responding to Economic Aftershocks", *OECD Journal on Budgeting*, Vol. 10, No. 2, OECD Publishing.

Silva, J. da (2008), "Local Governments in Portugal", *Urban Public Economics Review*, No. 9, Departamento de Economía Aplicada, Universidad de Santiago de Compostela.

Sorbe, S. (2012), "Portugal: Assessing the Risks About the Speed of Fiscal Consolidation in an Uncertain Environment", *OECD Economics Department Working Papers*, forthcoming

Statistics Portugal (2011), "Excessive Deficit Procedure, First Notification 2011", 31 March.

Sutherland, D., R. Price and I. Joumard (2005), "Fiscal Rules for Sub-central Governments: Design and Impact", *OECD Economics Department Working Papers*, No. 465, OECD Publishing.

Sutherland, D., P. Hoeller and R. Merola (2012), "Fiscal Consolidation: Part 1. How Much is Needed and How to Reduce Debt to a Prudent Level?", *OECD Economics Department Working Papers*, No. 932, OECD Publishing.

Veiga, L.G. (2010), "Determinants of the Assignment of EU Funds to Portuguese Municipalities", *NIPE Working Papers*, No. 11, Universidade do Minho.

Veiga, L and F. Veiga (2011), "Intergovernmental Fiscal Transfers as Pork Barrel", *Public Choice*, No. 110, Springer.

ANNEX 1.A1

Sensitivity of stochastic simulation results

This annex presents the sensitivity of the stochastic simulation results shown in Figure 1.2 and in Figure 6 of the Assessment and Recommendations to different assumptions regarding the fiscal multiplier and potential growth.

Figure 1.A1.1. **Sensitivity analysis: Fiscal multiplier of 0.5 (instead of 1)**

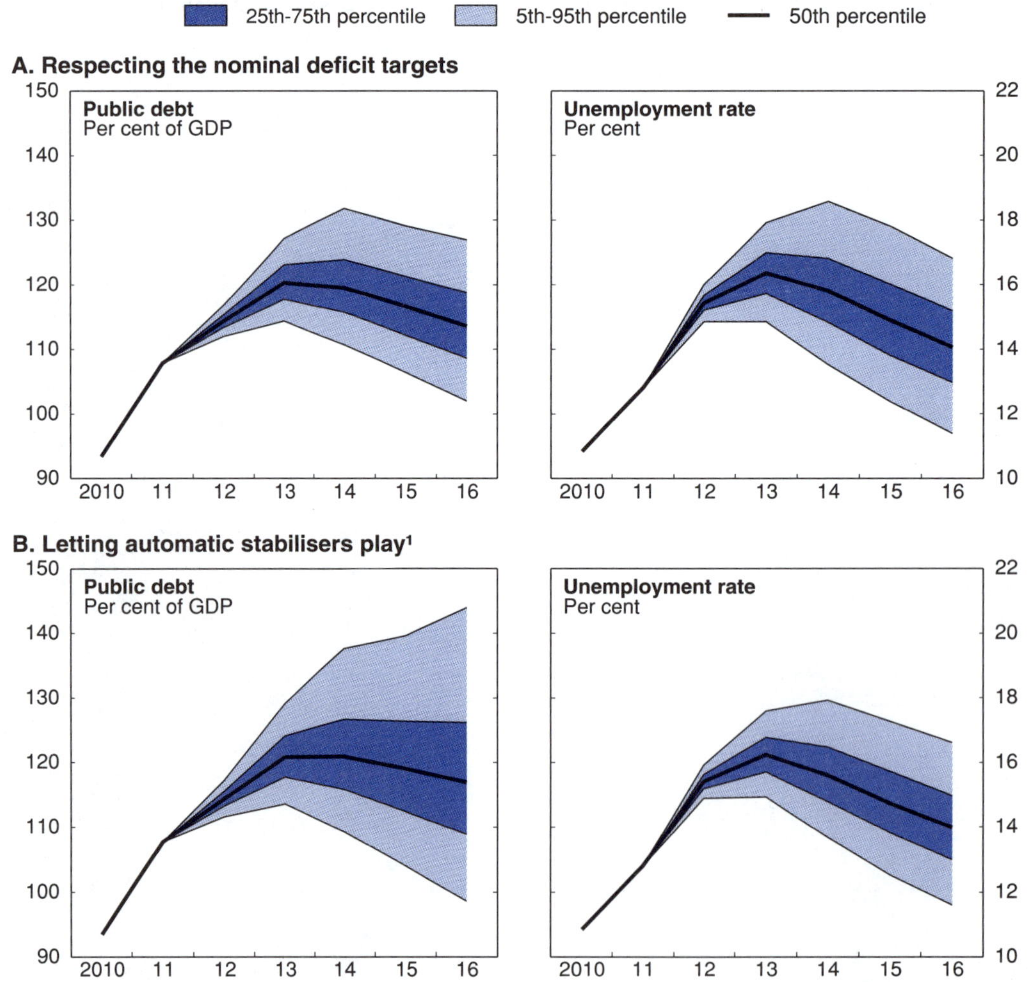
25th-75th percentile
5th-95th percentile
50th percentile
A. Respecting the nominal deficit targets
Public debt
Per cent of GDP
Unemployment rate
Per cent
150
140
130
120
110
100
90
22
20
18
16
14
12
10
2010 11 12 13 14 15 16
B. Letting automatic stabilisers play¹
Public debt
Per cent of GDP
Unemployment rate
Per cent

1. Respecting the structural primary deficit targets.

Source: S. Sorbe (2012), "Portugal: Assessing the Risks about the Speed of Fiscal Consolidation in an Uncertain Environment", *OECD Economics Department Working Papers*, forthcoming.

StatLink http://dx.doi.org/10.1787/888932669990

Figure 1.A1.2. **Sensitivity analysis: Average potential growth over 2012-16 of +1% (instead of +0.3%)**

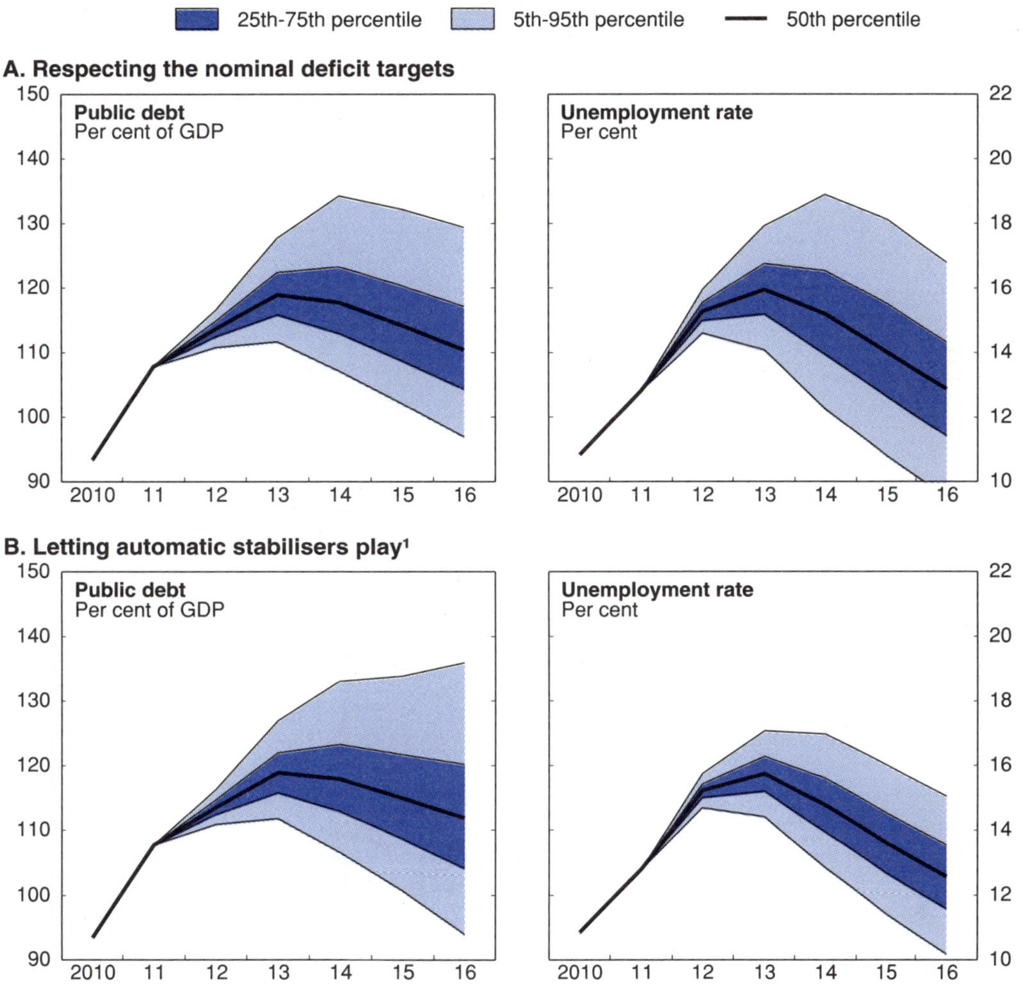
25th-75th percentile
5th-95th percentile
50th percentile
A. Respecting the nominal deficit targets
Public debt
Per cent of GDP
Unemployment rate
Per cent
B. Letting automatic stabilisers play[1]
Public debt
Per cent of GDP
Unemployment rate
Per cent
150
140
130
120
110
100
90
22
20
18
16
14
12
10
2010
11
12
13
14
15
16

1. Respecting the structural primary deficit targets.

Source: S. Sorbe (2012), "Portugal: Assessing the Risks about the Speed of Fiscal Consolidation in an Uncertain Environment", *OECD Economics Department Working Papers*, forthcoming.

StatLink http://dx.doi.org/10.1787/888932670009

Chapter 2

Rebalancing the economy and returning to growth through job creation and better capital allocation

Low growth and huge current account deficits have characterised the Portuguese economy over the past decade. Easy credit in global markets, combined with the absence of incentives to limit loan-to-deposit ratios until recently, made it possible to finance internationally high levels of consumption and investment relative to gross domestic product (GDP) through over reliance of the banking sector on wholesale funding. This led to high households' and firms' indebtedness and made banks vulnerable to shifts in investor sentiment. However, investment and credit were mostly directed to sheltered sectors, giving rise to an oversized road infrastructure, electricity generation capacity and housing stock. Weaknesses in labour market institutions further held back productivity and hampered wage adjustment, making it harder to gain cost competitiveness.

The deleveraging process set in motion by the loss of access to foreign financing is helping to rapidly reduce external deficits, but also has the potential to generate a damaging credit contraction, which enhances the importance of alternative financing strategies for firms, such as greater reliance on equity. To restore growth, Portugal needs to foster the reallocation of both labour and capital, essentially towards the tradable sector. Building on recent policy initiatives or commitments, this will require reforming public policies that have long distorted investment allocation, ensuring that banks adequately recognise and provision problematic loans and, on the employment front, reducing labour market segmentation and increasing targeted training. Reforms in wage setting, labour taxation, unemployment benefits and activation policies will foster job creation, thus enhancing output growth while avoiding high unemployment becoming entrenched and threatening social cohesion.

The crisis made imbalances unsustainable

After a lost decade, the Portuguese economy has embarked on a challenging process of economic adjustment and reform. Over 2001-10, real GDP growth averaged a meagre 0.6%, and unemployment almost tripled. Labour market institutions have held back productivity growth and hampered wage restraint, damaging external competitiveness. An array of product market inefficiencies and rents, especially in sheltered sectors, also hurt productivity and competitiveness, not least by distorting investment allocation. Insufficient risk perception allowed excessively high consumption and investment to be intermediated by domestic banks through international wholesale debt markets, especially as there were no incentives, such as a target for the loan-to-deposit ratio, to slow down lending until recently. Combined with poor export performance, this led to high external deficits and indebtedness. Despite a growing tax burden, public debt has also increased markedly, reflecting chronic difficulties in managing and controlling public expenditure, of which government-directed investment projects are a good example.

While many of these problems have been long identified and discussed (*e.g.* Blanchard, 2007), the global financial and sovereign debt crises have made them more acute and, when external private financing dried up, unsustainable. Since May 2011, Portugal has been steadfastly implementing an ambitious three-year European Union-International Monetary Fund (EU-IMF) financial assistance programme. It is important to ensure that the inevitable short-run costs of the on-going macro-financial adjustment do not degenerate into a deeper recession, and that continued structural reform efforts help to minimise the risk of unemployment becoming structural and lay the ground for sustained and balanced growth. After outlining how imbalances built up, this chapter discusses policies to rebalance the economy and return to growth, focusing on restoring the banking system to health, fostering efficient investment allocation and creating more and better jobs through improved labour market performance.

Macroeconomic imbalances have grown larger over the past decade

The very high current account deficits, of almost 10% of GDP on average during 2001-10, led to a sharp deterioration of the international investment position from –39% of GDP at end-2000 to –107% ten years later. This was reflected in the growing indebtedness of households and firms (Figure 2.1). Portugal lost substantial export market share until 2005, with no signs of any significant recovery until 2011, while imports were fuelled by high private consumption and (to a lesser extent) investment (Figure 2.2). After some ten years of persistent, though moderate, real appreciation, cost competitiveness essentially stagnated around the mid-2000s and did not start to recover until 2010, despite rising unemployment (Figure 2.3).

Figure 2.1. **Financial debt**[1]
Per cent of GDP

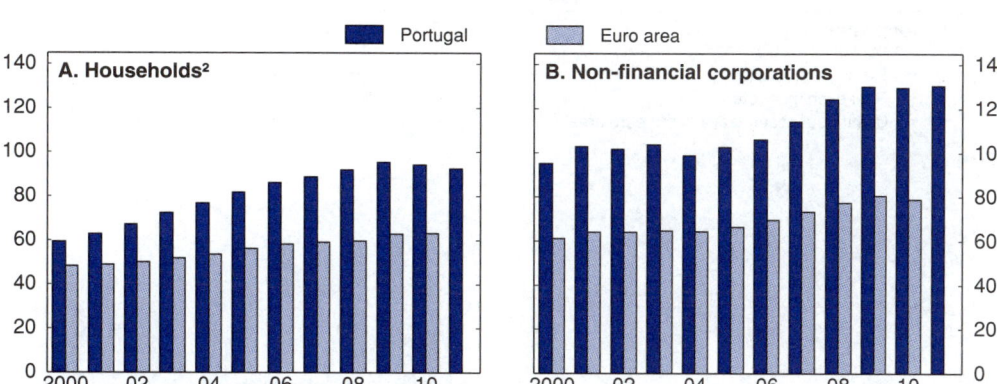

1. Loans plus securities other than shares.
2. Including non-profit institutions serving households.
Source: Eurostat (2012), "Economy and Finance", Eurostat Database, May.
StatLink http://dx.doi.org/10.1787/888932670028

Figure 2.2. **Private consumption and gross fixed capital formation**
Per cent of GDP

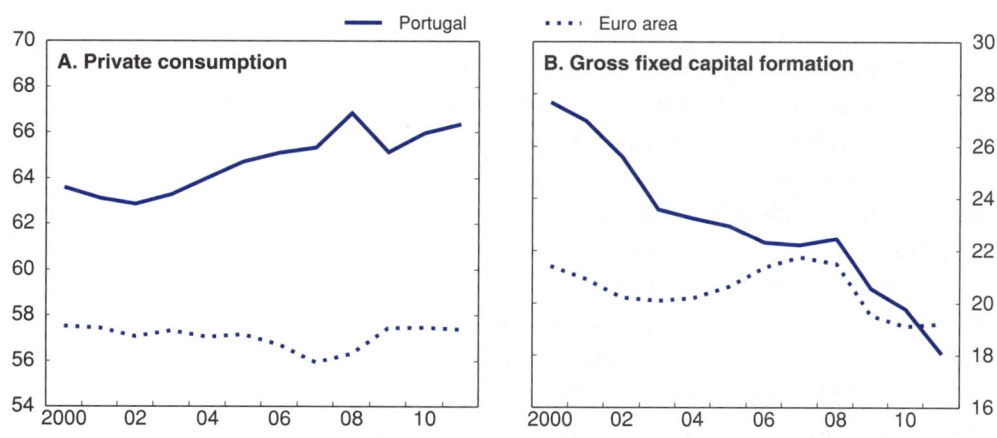

Source: Eurostat (2012), "Economy and Finance", Eurostat Database, May.
StatLink http://dx.doi.org/10.1787/888932670047

A highly inefficient labour market, where poor institutions predate the crisis, has weighed both on wage and productivity developments. Despite soaring unemployment since 2000, significant downward adjustment of private sector real wages only started in 2011 (Figure 2.3). Explanations for this include widespread administrative extension of collective agreements, long-lasting unemployment benefits (especially for older workers) and pervasive labour market segmentation, all of which cossets insiders and places the burden of adjustment on the fringe of temporary workers (Marques et al., 2009; Centeno and Novo, 2012). Large minimum wage increases in 2006-11 further worsened matters. Until 2010, there was no consistent policy of wage restraint in the public sector, which has some influence on private wage-setting (Lamo et al., 2008). Poor labour market institutions have also hampered productivity. Segmentation limits the mobility of permanent workers, and thus the quality of their job matches, and discourages human capital accumulation by temporary workers (Centeno and Novo, 2012). Administrative extension stifles competition between firms, as dominant firms use it as a way to exclude new competitors.

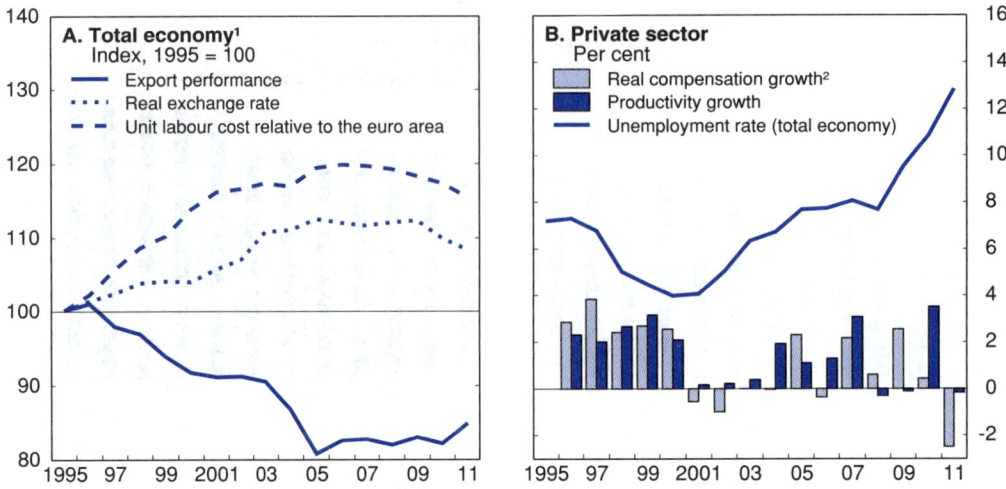

Figure 2.3. **Developments in cost competitiveness**

1. Export performance is the ratio between export volumes and export markets for total goods and services. The real exchange rate is a harmonised competitiveness indicator based on unit labour cost indices.
2. Compensation per worker in the private sector deflated by the harmonised consumer price index.

Source: Bank of Portugal and OECD (2012), *OECD Economic Outlook: Statistics and Projections* (database), May.

StatLink http://dx.doi.org/10.1787/888932670066

Though declining relative to GDP, investment has remained above the euro area average for most of the past decade (Figure 2.2), but its allocation has failed to spur productivity growth. A continued emphasis on government-promoted transport infrastructure, with both traditional public capital formation and public-private partnerships (PPP) adding to the substantial investment from the 1990s, likely accounts for more than half of the excess of the share of non-residential construction (other buildings and structures) relative to the euro area (Figure 2.4). In 2000-09, public capital formation, mostly non-residential construction, was on average 1 percentage point of GDP higher than in the euro area, and an almost as large differential has been estimated for PPP investment flows (Kappeler and Nemoz, 2010), mainly road projects (see Chapter 1).

As a result of distorted incentives for homeownership and poor rental market performance, housing investment remained skewed towards new dwellings (rather than renovation). Although declining, investment further expanded the housing stock, already large at the turn of the century. Amidst shrinking investment in most sectors (though, in the case of construction and others, from a high starting point), energy stands out as an exception (Figure 2.4), with investment increasing from 0.6% of GDP in 2000 to 1.6% in 2009 (against a stable 0.6% for the 20 EU countries for which data is available). This increase has been partly due to incentives for electricity production which caused a surge in wind farms (with concomitant network expansion) and, to a smaller extent, in other generation technologies, leading to excessive production capacity.

Financial sector developments have mirrored these trends in indebtedness and investment allocation. Large-scale resort to international wholesale debt markets has filled a yawning gap between credit and deposits in the domestic banking system. Portuguese banks had the fourth highest euro area credit-to-deposit ratio in 2009 (after Estonia, Ireland and Slovenia), and the fourth largest increase since 2000 (Beck et al., 2000). In addition, the allocation of credit to construction-related activities has been reinforced, to the detriment of tradable sectors (Figure 2.5).

Figure 2.4. **Investment allocation by assets and sectors**[1]

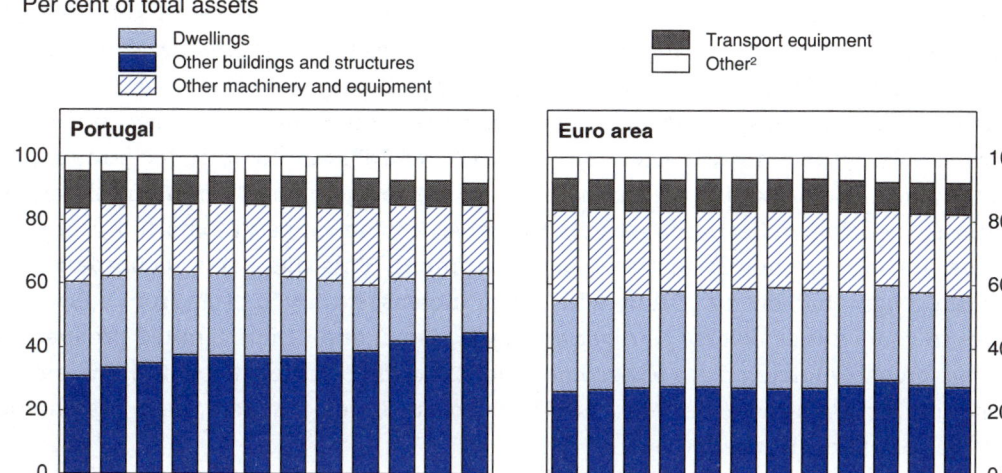

1. Gross fixed capital formation.
2. Cultivated and intangible fixed assets.
3. In real terms according to the NACE Revision 2 European Classification of Economic Activities.
Source: Eurostat (2012), "Economy and Finance", *Eurostat Database*, May.

StatLink ⟶ http://dx.doi.org/10.1787/888932670085

Figure 2.5. **Banking sector developments**

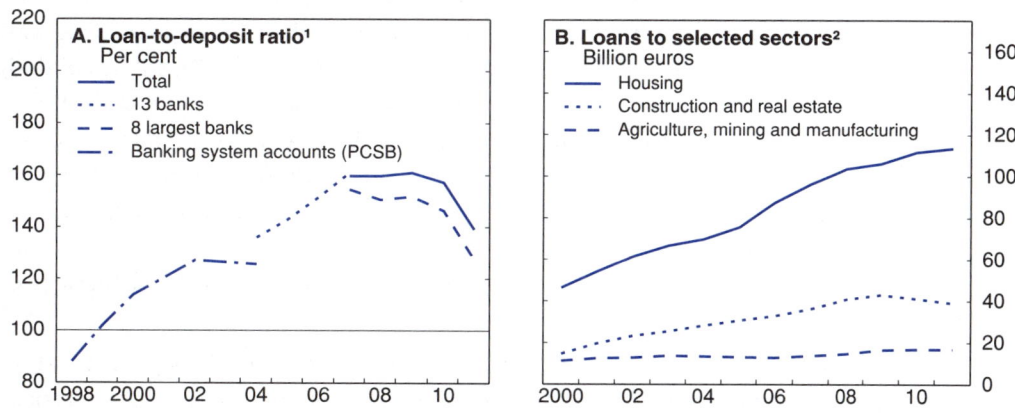

1. Based on International Accounting Standards (IAS) except for PCSB: *Plano de contas do sistema bancário*.
2. Loans to households and non-financial companies. Average of monthly data.
Source: Bank of Portugal.

StatLink ⟶ http://dx.doi.org/10.1787/888932670104

Wide-scale adjustment began in 2011

The correction of macroeconomic and financial imbalances started in earnest only in 2011. The gradual loss of access to foreign financing by the sovereign and domestic banks over the course of 2010 and early 2011 was increasingly replaced by official capital flows (Merler and Pisani-Ferry, 2012), mainly through Eurosystem financing and EU-IMF financial assistance. Despite sizeable terms-of-trade losses, the current account deficit narrowed substantially in 2011 (from 10% to 6.4% of GDP), due to both declining import volumes and a strong export performance. While the former stem from internal demand weakness, the latter reflects robust growth across a wide range of exported goods and services, most prominently in transport equipment. This has been accompanied by increased geographic diversification, with major increases (though often from a low base) in sales to countries as diverse as Algeria, Angola, Brazil and China. Limited prospects at home are arguably forcing firms to become more exported oriented. Recent improvements in cost competitiveness, especially vis-à-vis non euro area partners, have also helped export performance (Figure 2.3).

Unwinding macro-financial imbalances

Managing bank deleveraging to ensure adequate credit supply

Bank deleveraging is essential to reinforce financial stability and ease the return to wholesale market funding, and will accompany the necessary reduction of indebtedness of households and non-financial firms. Core Tier 1 ratios need to comply with targets set by the Bank of Portugal (9 and 10% at end-2011 and end-2012) and, for four of the largest banking groups, by the European Banking Authority (EBA) (9% by 30 June 2012, computed under slightly different and more demanding rules, plus a capital buffer for sovereign exposures). Further, the eight largest groups, accounting for 83% of the system's assets, are to reduce their loan-to-deposit ratios towards an indicative 120% target by end-2014. However, if pursued at too fast a pace, necessary bank deleveraging has the potential to threaten an adequate credit supply to viable firms and worsen recessionary dynamics.

Progress has been made in increasing Core Tier 1 ratios, through both numerator and denominator (Table 2.1). Among the eight largest banks, three already reached the 10% target in 2011 and a fourth one (covered by EBA requirements) has reached that target in 2012 with private funds only. The others, which include the three banks with the largest needs for sovereign capital buffers plus a smaller institution, have resorted to (or are expected to require) public support for recapitalisation, funded, apart from the state-owned Caixa Geral de Depósitos, under an EU-IMF programme facility of EUR 12 billion. The EBA sovereign buffer has been by far the most important determinant of increased capital needs (Table 2.1), largely reflecting banks' exposure to Portuguese sovereign debt, which surged in 2010. Other major determinants, dating from 2011 but with impacts on regulatory capital deferred until June 2012, have been the recognition of actuarial losses associated to the transfer of banks' pension funds to the general social security regime (see Assessment and Recommendations) and additional credit impairments under the Special Inspections Programme (see below).

Rules for bank recapitalisation with government funds should strike a balance between safeguarding taxpayers' interests, minimising the risk of political interference in credit allocation and creating incentives for private shareholders to reimburse public support as soon as feasible. Under Portuguese legislation, recently revised and compliant

Table 2.1. **Data on bank recapitalisation for the eight largest groups**
Million euros

A. Progress in Core Tier 1 ratios	End of period			
Bank of Portugal definition	2009	2010	2011	Jun-2012[1]
Core Tier 1 (CT1) capital (A)	21 591	22 631	25 283	30 457
CT1 increase due to conversion of non-core into core elements[2]	16	16	2 528	0
Other CT1 increases	3 990	1 024	124	5 174
Total capital requirements (B)	22 999	23 162	21 732	21 775
Core Tier 1 ratio (%) [A/(B*12.5)]	7.5	7.8	9.3	11.2

B. Increased Core Tier 1 needs and capitalisation measures to meet EBA targets

December 2011 to June 2012

Factors generating increased Core Tier 1 capital needs	5 681	Capitalisation measures	7 886
Shortfall in 31.12.2011 for an EBA CT1 ratio of 9% (excluding factors below)	523	Of private sources	1 236
Special Inspections Programme (deduction to 31.12.2011 CT1 capital)	436	Of public sources	6 650
Pension Funds transfer (deduction to 31.12.2011 CT1 capital)	962	Caixa Geral de Depósitos (shares plus CoCos)	1 650
Sovereign capital buffer (4 groups)	3 718	Private banks – shares[3]	500
Other	43	Private banks – CoCos[4]	4 500

1. Forecast.
2. Does not include repurchases of debt instruments.
3. Planned share capital increase underwritten by the Portuguese State, to be preferentially subscribed by private investors.
4. Of which EUR 200 million might be converted into shares if a planned share capital increase of that amount, to be preferentially subscribed by private investors, is not completed by 30 September 2012.

Source: Bank of Portugal.

with EU competition rules, the government can inject funds using either common equity or hybrid debt instruments, such as contingent convertible securities (CoCos). Shares will be bought or subscribed at a substantial discount relative to market prices and are entitled to a priority dividend, but confer no voting rights in ordinary management decisions (except for those shares in excess of 50% of total common equity, which is a relatively high threshold). Hybrid debt instruments can make up to 50% of eligible capital and will pay an interest rate initially set between 7 and 9.3%. This rate increases over time, which reinforces incentives to shorten the duration of public support. Banks requiring public funds must submit recapitalisation plans containing *inter alia* their intended business model, governance reforms and the schedule for public divestment. In case of non-compliance (assessed by the Bank of Portugal) or, in any case, after five years, all remaining public capitalisation instruments (shares or others) will be converted into shares with full voting rights.

Based on the recapitalisation plans submitted by the three largest banks requiring public support (two private and one state-owned), the authorities made available more than EUR 6.5 billion of public funds, of which up to 5 billion from the EU-IMF programme facility (Table 2.1), allowing the banks concerned to exceed both EBA and Bank of Portugal minimum capital requirements by a considerable margin. While funds in the two private banks have so far been injected through contingent convertible securities (amounting to EUR 4.5 billion and paying an initial interest rate of 8.5%), the government may also end up with a sizeable equity position in those institutions, essentially corresponding to the remainder of forthcoming rights issues that existing private shareholders leave unsubscribed. In these and any future recapitalisation operations, the authorities should ensure that the potential costs to taxpayers and the final beneficiaries of the funds are fully transparent, so as to reduce moral hazard and maintain public support (IMF, 2009). Further, as envisaged, the authorities should keep the remainder of the EUR 12 billion envelope for further capital increases if needed, even after 2012 capital targets are met. This will help to minimise the risk of credit rationing, if losses from credit impairments, likely to stay high or even increase in the near future, put downward pressure on capital and hence on risk-weighted assets as well.

Banks have been reducing their loan-to-deposit ratios, which for the banking system as whole fell from a peak of 167% in June 2010 to 140% in December 2011 (Figure 2.6). The ratio for the eight largest banks as a whole was reduced likewise, to around 130%. However, there is considerable dispersion across banks. While five of those eight banks are already below, or very close to, the 120% indicative target, the other three were still above 140% at end-2011.

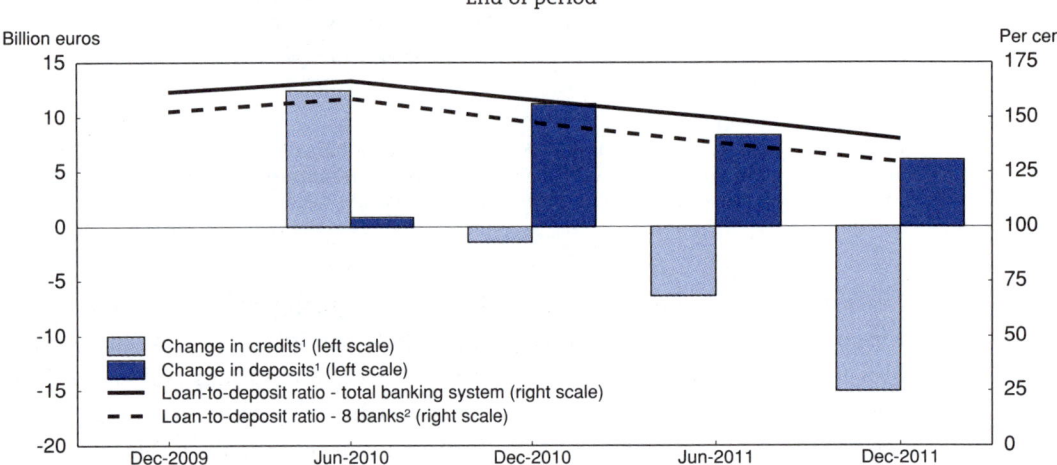

Figure 2.6. **Recent developments in banks' loan-to-deposit ratio**
End of period

1. Since the previous semester.
2. The definition of the loan-to-deposit ratio relevant for the 120% indicative target is slightly different from the one depicted (generally 1-2 percentage points higher).

Source: Bank of Portugal.

StatLink ⟶ http://dx.doi.org/10.1787/888932670123

Deposits have been growing vigorously since mid-2010, and account for most of the progress so far in reducing loan-to-deposit ratios. Contributions to deposit growth initially came from non-financial firms and non-monetary financial institutions but, in 2011, mainly from private individuals and general government. Attracted by higher rates on deposits, households have adjusted the composition of their financial asset portfolios away from other savings instruments managed within banks' financial groups (*e.g.* by investment funds or insurance companies) or non-tradable public debt (saving certificates). Unspent funds from the EU-IMF programme have enabled general government deposits to more than double in 2011. However, the potential for further deposit growth will wane over time. Developments in early 2012 suggest that deposits by private individuals, though still posting robust year-on-year growth, are slowing down, while the more volatile deposits by firms are decreasing.

Over the course of 2011, a progressively larger share of the loan-to-deposit ratio decline has come from the numerator, not only through growing credit impairments (further addressed below) and credit portfolio sales, but also as a result of considerable reduction of loans to firms and households. Overall developments in domestic bank loans nonetheless hide stark differences in financing conditions across non-financial firms (Figure 2.7). Total credit granted by either resident or non-resident entities has displayed a more benign trend, as some private sector large firms and non-financial holdings have managed to increase their external financing (Bank of Portugal, 2011). Lending by domestic banks to state-owned enterprises (SOE) outside general government has steeply increased, reflecting continued operational losses and the need to replace non-resident lenders in rolling over maturing debt, though it should be borne in mind that those enterprises only account for little more than 5% of outstanding loans by the resident financial sector to nonfinancial corporations. In contrast, small and medium-sized enterprises (SME), traditionally more reliant on resident lenders, especially banks, have witnessed major falls in credit. This is in line with credit constraints reported in sectoral surveys, which are highest in construction, but have been increasing also in manufacturing and services. These constraints also hamper the ability of SMEs to tap supports for internationalisation and research and development (R&D) co-financed by EU funds.

Figure 2.7. **Credit to non-financial firms**
Annual change, per cent

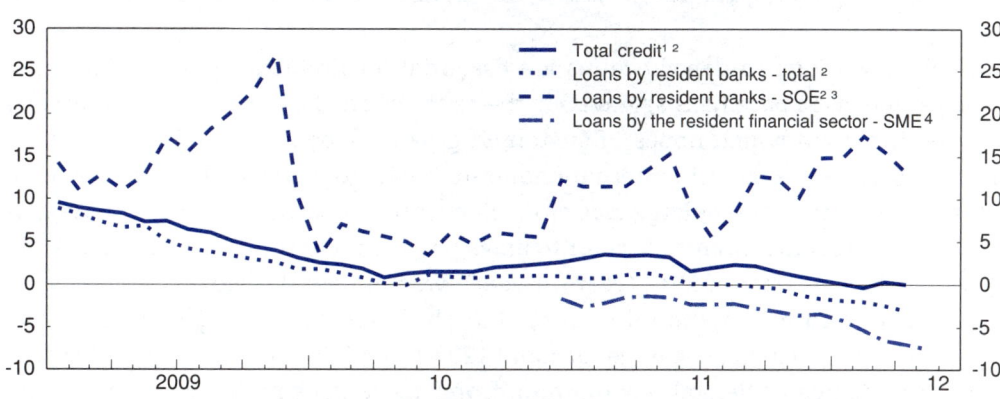

1. On a consolidated basis, covering loans, debt securities and trade credits. Includes credit granted by non-resident entities.
2. Figures are adjusted for securitisation operations, reclassifications, write-offs/write-downs, exchange rate changes and price revaluations. Whenever relevant, the figures are additionally adjusted for credit portfolio sales, as well as for other operations with no impact on non-financial corporations' effective financing.
3. State-owned enterprises (SOE) which do not consolidate under general government.
4. Includes loans to small and medium-sized enterprises (SME) by monetary and non-monetary financial institutions. Year-on-year rate of change.
Source: Bank of Portugal (2012), *Indicadores de Conjuntura* and *Boletim Estatístico*, June.

StatLink http://dx.doi.org/10.1787/888932670142

To ease pressure on deposit rates, the Bank of Portugal introduced in November 2011, and reinforced in April 2012, additional capital requirements for deposits paying high rates, currently defined as those in excess of a 225-300 basis point spread (depending on term) over a market reference rate (often the Euribor). Helped by bond issuance operations under a EUR 35 billion state guarantee facility (eligible as Eurosystem collateral), as well as by further measures to increase collateral availability taken in February 2012, Portuguese banks took advantage of the two recent three-year European Central Bank (ECB) long-term refinancing operations to both extend the maturity of their Eurosystem funding and increase its overall amount (Figure 2.8). However, apart from some decrease in interest rates on new loans to non-financial firms (rates which remain nonetheless very high), financing conditions in the economy have not eased yet. Indeed, bank lending surveys suggest that some further tightening of credit standards in loans to firms took place in the first quarter of 2012 and was likely to continue in the second quarter (especially as regards long-term lending), in contrast to loan demand, which was expected to recover mildly.

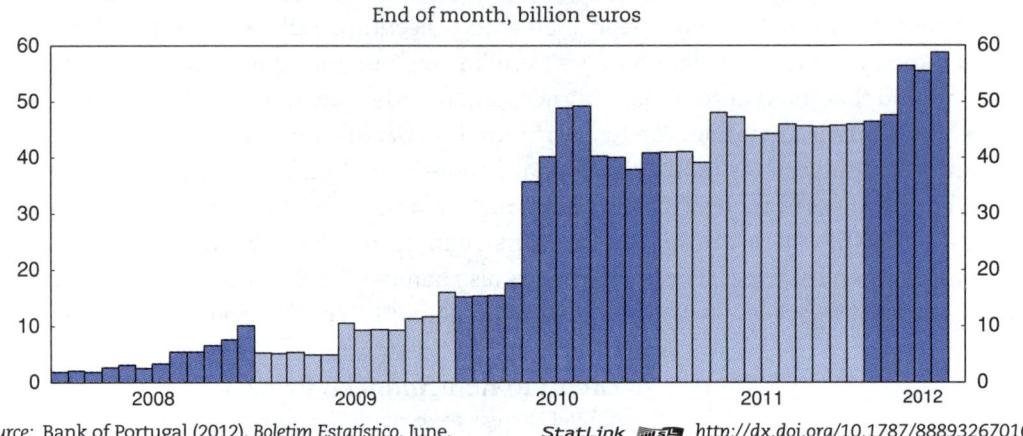

Figure 2.8. **Provision of Eurosystem liquidity to Portuguese banks**
End of month, billion euros

Source: Bank of Portugal (2012), Boletim Estatístico, June.   StatLink ⟶ http://dx.doi.org/10.1787/888932670161

While lower loan-to-deposit ratios are essential for financial stability, deleveraging pursued at too fast a pace risks aggravating the contraction of credit and economic activity. Exporting firms, on which hopes of sustained growth depend, are vulnerable to credit constraints, as involvement in international trade tends to increase the need for working capital and investment to enlarge capacity will eventually become necessary. The growth of loans by the resident financial sector to exporting companies has declined markedly to 1.8% in the first quarter of 2012 (year-on-year), with no similar slow down in nominal exports. The authorities should ensure that the pace of convergence towards the loan-to-deposit ratio indicative target of about 120% by end-2014 does not thwart economic activity. The degree of flexibility stemming from the target's indicative nature is made more important by the fact that those banks further away from the target have on average a larger weight of loans to firms in their portfolios.

Fostering credit reallocation and a smaller reliance on debt financing

Deleveraging should be accompanied by the removal of distortions to credit reallocation across sectors, to enable productivity-enhancing shifts in investment composition. While distortions in housing and energy are discussed below, financing pressures from SOE (Figure 2.7), mostly in non-tradable sectors, are hampering reallocation, which underlines the importance of on-going efforts to improve their operational performance (Chapter 1). When appropriate, cancelling or buying back PPP road projects (Chapter 1) would also have a payoff in terms of reallocating credit away from construction.

On the credit supply side, it is essential that banks refrain from "ever-greening" problematic loans, as the ensuing protracted loss recognition would tend to depress productivity growth and slow down recovery. To this end, several welcome steps have been recently taken by the Bank of Portugal. Supervisory capabilities have been strengthened following the Special Inspections Programme, which examined on-site the credit portfolios and stress-testing methods of the eight largest banking groups (with overall positive results). Further on-site inspections are planned, which is welcome. Faced with major sales of banks' non-performing loans to outside vehicles (*e.g.* venture capital funds, often headquartered abroad), the central bank has required detailed information reporting and imposed high risk weights on banks' exposures to those vehicles, which may be used to defer losses in case of insufficient haircuts. Further, banks have also been required to identify all instances of restructured loans (even if still performing) due to financial difficulties of the borrower. In this respect, the recent corporate insolvency law amendments, as well as the extra-judicial conciliation framework now being finalised, are expected to facilitate the early rescue of viable firms. The authorities should make data on restructured loans public and continue to use supervisory tools to promote swift recognition of bad loans. As discussed above, this may make it necessary to provide banks with more capital support.

Credit reallocation to viable SMEs would also be promoted by reversing the 2011 steep increase in the prudential risk weight attached to loans granted under government-sponsored credit lines. These loans benefit from a private sector credit guarantee, part of which enjoys in turn a government fund counter-guarantee, amounting in general to 37.5% of the loan. As the fund providing the counter-guarantee is by its legal setup considered to have the same risk as a credit institution for prudential purposes, exposures to the fund (*i.e.* 37.5% of the guaranteed loans) saw their risk weights soar from 20 to 100% in 2011, as did exposures to credit institutions, when Portuguese sovereign debt lost investment grade. Higher risk weights made those loans less attractive to banks. The authorities could reconsider that aspect of the legal setup of the counter-guarantee fund, thus allowing for lower risk weights on loans under SME credit lines.

As deleveraging proceeds, companies will need to become less dependent on credit and more reliant on equity, of either national or foreign origin, which *inter alia* will make the economy more resilient to financial crises (Ahrend and Goujard, 2012). Foreign direct investment (FDI) accounts for a below-average share of total external liabilities (16% in 2010, against 26% across the OECD), notwithstanding low statutory barriers. In the past, the prospect of foreign investors taking majority stakes at large companies was sometimes regarded with reservations (Ministry of Finance, 2011), in sharp contrast to an attitude of often benign neglect towards high current account deficits. Yet FDI can be an important source of technology transfer and, in times of tight internal credit, may also ease access to external market financing. Opening up the economy and reducing external imbalances are important goals under the EU-IMF programme.

Portuguese firms have a high debt-to-equity ratio, which increases their vulnerability to downturns and deteriorating operational earnings (IMF, 2012). Reluctance to opening shareholder control to new partners has been a long-standing barrier to capital market entry by many SMEs. Additionally, the corporate income tax regime has long favoured debt finance over equity finance, a bias worsened in recent years by the introduction and subsequent increase of a tax rate surcharge for profits above certain thresholds (*derrama estadual*) in the context of fiscal consolidation, as well as by the increased taxation of capital gains on equity shares (since 2010), though the latter is welcome from an income distribution viewpoint (OECD, 2010a). An allowance for corporate equity, introduced in 2008, has so far been scantily availed of, possibly because its scope is limited to SMEs, among other constraints. The authorities should take further steps to alleviate the debt bias embedded in the tax system. One among several possibilities would be to limit interest payments deductibility, and use the ensuing increase in revenue to reduce the corporate tax rate.

Removing distortions to investment allocation

Housing market reforms to improve capital allocation and increase labour mobility

Rental market and tax policies excessively favoured homeownership and biased capital allocation

Portugal has a housing stock among the highest in the OECD area, mostly owner-occupied (Figure 2.9). Over the past decade, investment in new dwellings, though on a declining trend, expanded the stock per inhabitant by around 15%, with an increasing share of vacant homes (13% of the stock in 2011, which is relatively high by European standards; OTB, 2010). Around one-third of the stock requires renovation, as investment has been largely slanted to new

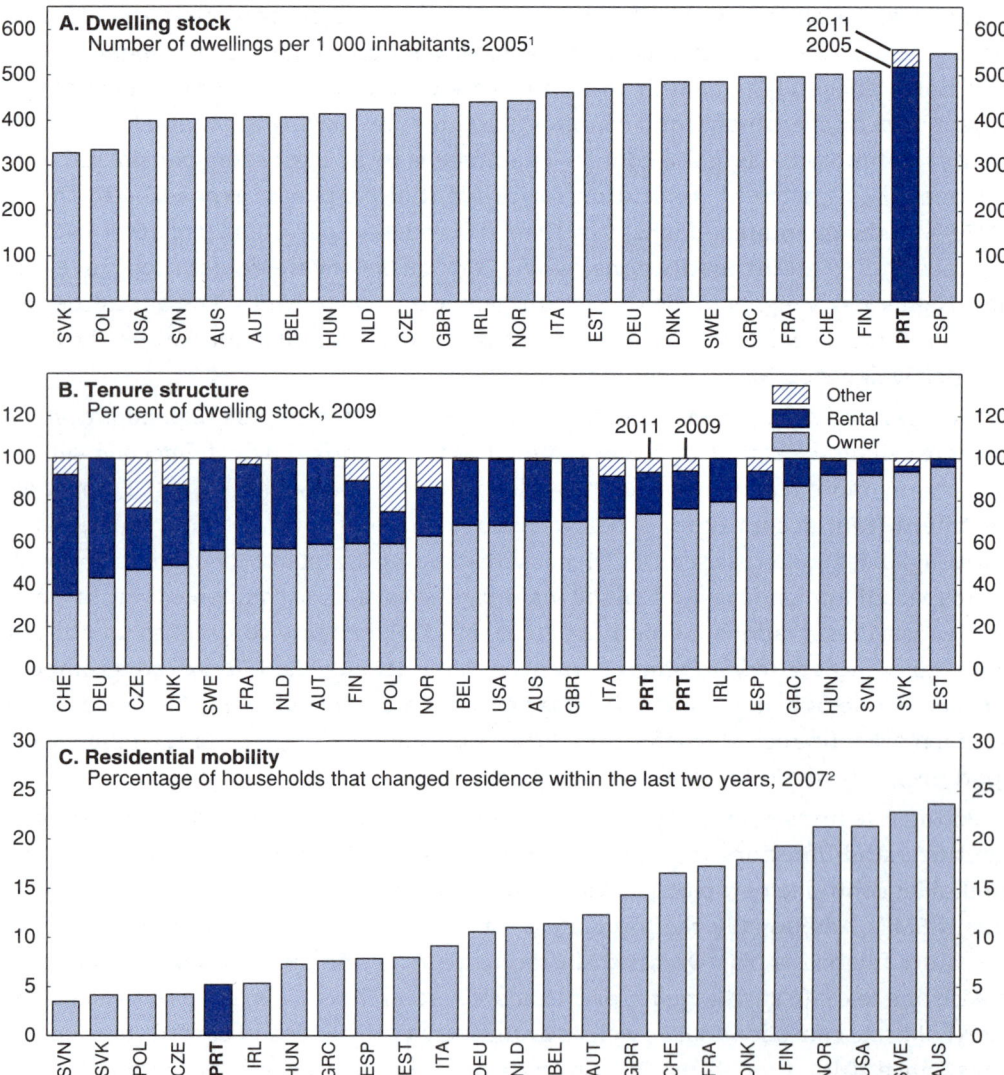

Figure 2.9. **Housing structure in international comparison**

1. 2001 for Belgium, Czech Republic and Greece; 2003 for Australia and Italy; 2004 for France and Switzerland.
2. The low mobility rate in some Eastern European countries does not seem reasonable and may reflect problems with the underlying data. However, this is difficult to verify as there is no alternative data source.

Source: D. Andrews, A. Caldera Sánchez and Å. Johansson (2011), "Housing Markets and Structural Policies in OECD Countries", *OECD Economics Department Working Papers*, No. 836 and INE (2011), *Censos 2011, Resultados provisórios*, Instituto Nacional de Estatística.

StatLink http://dx.doi.org/10.1787/888932670180

construction (AECOPS, 2009). The increasing level of homeownership went along with growing indebtedness of households (around 80% of loans to households were for house purchase – Figure 2.1). It also helps to explain low residential mobility, as homeowners are generally found to be less mobile than tenants (Caldera Sánchez and Andrews, 2011). In turn, this can be an obstacle to efficient job-matching.

The increase in homeownership in Portugal over recent decades is partly due to ageing and rising disposable income but also importantly to easier access to credit and to rental market and tax policies, as in other OECD countries (Andrews and Caldera Sánchez, 2011). Poor rental policies have resulted in a malfunctioning and small rental sector (20% of dwellings in 2011, which is below that in most OECD countries). Regulations governing tenant-landlord relationships favour tenants more than in other countries (Andrews et al., 2011). In particular, long and cumbersome eviction procedures have been a major hurdle to the supply of rental housing. Long-standing rent controls for older contracts (33% of the total, 70% of which paying rents below EUR 100 per month) create rigidities, as tenants are reluctant to give up tenure security and below-market rents. This has strongly discouraged investment in dwelling maintenance, which has also been held back by red tape and complex regulations for renovation. Limited supply and high risk for landlords have resulted in high rents for newer contracts. The preferential tax treatment of owner-occupied housing is likely to have helped to divert capital from more productive investments. Imputed rents are not taxed and, until 2011, mortgage interest and principal payments were tax deductible. For most properties, taxable values under recurrent immovable property taxes have long lagged behind market value and significant exemptions have persisted, though progress is now underway (see below).

Thorough implementation of reforms is essential to increase the supply of rental housing

The new urban lease legislation, expected to come into force after the summer, is an important step forward in balancing rights and obligations of landlords and tenants as regards eviction procedures of non-complying tenants. Until now, landlords had to go through the courts and enter eviction procedures (*acção executiva*), the latter alone taking sixteen months on average. The new legislation creates an extrajudicial procedure which aims at reducing average eviction time to three months. If the tenant opposes the eviction, the ensuing judicial process will have an urgent nature. The efficacy of the new procedures is still uncertain and the authorities should be ready to take corrective actions, if warranted, to ensure that both extrajudicial and judicial processes effectively decrease the eviction time of non-complying tenants, as envisaged.

The new legislation also tackles rent controls, an area where past reforms have largely failed. Under the new rules, old contracts (those predating 1990) can be renegotiated and, in case of no agreement, landlords can choose between contract termination with compensation and a five-year contract with an updated rent subject to an annual maximum of 6.7% of the property taxable value, after which full liberalisation applies. However, wide-ranging exceptions apply, for both residential and non-residential leases. Residential tenants who are aged 65 and over (60% of the pre-1990 residential leases, which amounts to 20% of total residential lease contracts) or have a level of disability over 60% cannot be forced to leave even after five years, and the above rent ceiling will persist. This lacks means-testing. Except for low-income old or disabled people, the authorities should ensure that after this five-year transitory period any ceiling to these rents is no longer below market values.

Another exception concerns leases to low-income tenants, which cannot in general be terminated during a transitional five-year period and will benefit during this period from a lower and income-dependent rent ceiling. Though rent liberalisation after those five years is welcome, low-income tenants of all ages will need support once the transitory period expires, and instruments to that end should be announced as soon as possible. Well-designed portable rent allowances might be considered, as these do not seem to hinder residential mobility (Andrews *et al.*, 2011). Exceptions to the possibility of contract termination also cover broadly-defined small businesses, implying that many retailers will benefit for five years from the fact that the transitional 6.7% rent ceiling will often keep rent levels below current market values, which distorts competition. If a significant divergence between market and transitional regulated rents persists, the authorities should shorten the transitory period, raise the ceiling or adopt a narrower definition of small businesses.

In a welcome move, the authorities have also changed legislation to simplify administrative procedures for renovation. The recent changes in both urban renovation and rental legislation are likely to give a much-needed boost to rental supply, made all the more necessary by the likely increase in demand stemming from household deleveraging and tighter credit. Currently vacant homes are expected to play a part in raising rental supply, especially given their upcoming higher property tax costs (updated taxable values in general plus a much higher tax rate for vacant dwellings). To foster this process, the existing financing incentives for renovation works, which are currently being re-evaluated by the authorities, should be focused on dwellings for rental.

Remove the preferential tax treatment of owner-occupied housing

Since 2011, there have been welcome steps to reduce the preferential tax treatment of owner-occupied housing. Mortgage interest deductibility is being gradually phased out and that of mortgage principal has been eliminated. Rent deductibility is also being phased out, although at a slower pace. As for recurrent taxes on immovable property, the authorities are carrying out a general updating of urban property taxable values, to be completed by end-2012, have plans for regular updating in the future, and have significantly reduced temporary tax exemptions for principal owner-occupied dwellings. The authorities should proceed with implementation according to planned deadlines and, as recurrent tax proceeds gradually increase, reduce reliance on the distorting real estate transaction tax, by levying it only on the initial transactions of property. In a second step, the transaction tax could be replaced by value-added tax (VAT) (OECD, 2010a). Even though Portugal compares favourably with other European countries regarding housing transaction costs, the weight of taxes in the costs of purchasing a dwelling is somewhat higher than average (EMF, 2010).

Addressing rents in the energy sector to foster efficient capital allocation and improve competitiveness

Regulatory interventions are granting unwarranted returns to electricity generators and distorting capital allocation

Opening the electricity sector to private initiative and competition and promoting renewable energy have been at the core of Portugal's energy policy since the mid-1990s. Electricity generation has been gradually opened to competition, though the previous incumbent, EDP – Energias de Portugal, still holds a high wholesale market share (around two-thirds in 2011). Transmission and distribution have been unbundled. Transmission is carried out by a single company, REN – Rede Eléctrica Nacional, and distribution remains a virtual monopoly of EDP. An Iberian electricity market has been implemented, aided by an increase in interconnection capacity. The retail sector has two segments, a competitive liberalised market (47% of total power supplied in 2011) and a market with regulated tariffs, which are being phased out. EDP is the chief supplier in the latter segment (as last-resort supplier) and is also the largest player in the former, with a market share of 42% in terms of volume, against around 25% for each of its two main competitors (and 80% in terms of the number of clients, against around 15% for the second firm).

In recent years, Portugal has become a leader in Europe in terms of renewables (Figure 2.10), largely due to the rapid growth of wind power from below 1% of gross electricity production in 2000 to 19% in 2011. Progress in harnessing renewable sources plays a major role in Portugal's contribution to the EU efforts to reduce greenhouse gas emissions and to strengthen energy security. Portugal's emissions have been declining since 2005 and, partly because of the economic crisis, in 2009 were already slightly below their Kyoto Protocol target for 2008-12. However, the integration of such large amounts of wind power in the electricity system requires, due to its intermittent nature, excess supply capacity of other sources that can quickly respond when there is no wind (*e.g.* thermal plants) or take advantage of excessive wind power when demand is low (*e.g.* pumped hydro storage) (Lopes and Gata, 2005). Six new dams are to be constructed by 2017, three of which with pumped storage. Existing thermal plants are operating significantly below their full capacity. Therefore, there is some excess generation capacity, all the more so given the currently foreseen reduction of electricity consumption.

Figure 2.10. **Share of renewables in electricity production**
Per cent of total gross electricity production, 2010

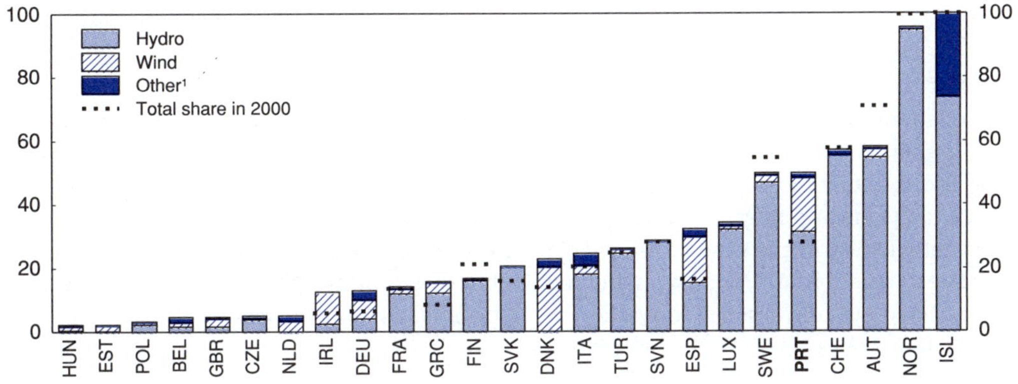

1. Geothermal, solar, tide/wave/ocean, gas from biomass, liquid biomass, solid biomass and renewable municipal waste.
Source: IEA (2012), "Electricity and Heat Generation", *IEA Electricity Information Statistics* (database), International Energy Agency, May.

StatLink http://dx.doi.org/10.1787/888932670199

Energy policy objectives, either environmental or concerning sector liberalisation, have been largely pursued through support to producers (Box 2.1). Most generators currently benefit either from feed-in tariffs (*i.e.* a regulated above-market price at which all electricity produced is sold to the network) for renewables and cogeneration, or from financial mechanisms to ensure profitability for fossil-fuel power and large hydro plants. All these support mechanisms give generators a revenue per unit of electricity produced

> **Box 2.1. Support to electricity generators**
>
> Most electricity generators under the ordinary regulatory regime (fossil-fuel power and large hydroelectric plants) benefit either from financial mechanisms to ensure profitability or, more recently, from payments for availability:
>
> - Power Purchase Agreements (*Contratos de Aquisição de Energia*) were created in the mid-1990s with the launch of international tenders to open the sector to private investment. Plants under these long-term contracts supply their energy in exchange for a pre-established rate of return, which is independent of their effective generation.
> - The early termination in 2007 of Energias de Portugal's (EDP) Power Purchase Agreements, to facilitate liquidity in the Iberian market, was compensated with the Costs for the Preservation of Contractual Equilibrium (*Custos para a Manutenção do Equilíbrio Contratual*) mechanism. This guarantees that plants will be able to recoup the same profitability by selling production in the market as they would have obtained under the former contracts. The mechanism includes a fixed annuity, to be received for 20 years, meant to correspond to the estimated net present value of the previous contracts plus financial costs. This was done on unfavourable terms because future cash flows were discounted at a rate of around 5% (government bonds plus 0.25 percentage points) while the financial costs of the annuity are capitalised at a nominal rate of 7.55% (average cost of capital of the producer).
> - The Power Guarantee Mechanism (*Mecanismo de Garantia de Potência*) was established in 2010 to remunerate generators for providing stand-by capacity available to the system. It was granted as an incentive to investment (EUR 20 000 per megawatt per annum) but applied to already existing or licensed plants. In a welcome step, the authorities have recently discontinued this scheme, and committed to redesign future payments for availability.
>
> Producers under the special regime (renewables and cogeneration) benefit from the last-resort supplier obligation to buy all electricity they generate and from a pre-established feed-in tariff:
>
> - The feed-in tariffs paid to renewables are differentiated by technology and guaranteed for a fixed time frame (15 years in most cases). They take into account environmental benefits and are adjusted monthly for inflation.
> - Cogeneration benefits from a feed-in tariff paid on all production sold to the last-resort supplier plus an efficiency premium and a renewable energy premium. The feed-in tariff is indexed to inflation and to changes in the oil price and exchange rate. It is guaranteed for ten years and may be revised and extended for another ten years, but no time limit is established in the case of renewable cogeneration. Under this setup, the authorities have in recent months considerably reduced future remuneration for cogeneration so as to accelerate convergence to market-based pricing, which is welcome.

above the liberalised wholesale market price (Figure 2.11) and largely insulate them from market risks, such as those stemming from demand or price fluctuations. Supports are often excessively generous and hence cost-inefficient, distorting investment allocation, as argued above, and weighing beyond necessary on electricity costs and prices (see below).

In the case of renewables, feed-in tariffs are the key support instrument. They were very effective in stimulating the development of renewable electricity, especially from wind, but too costly in some cases. Renewables support expenditures in Portugal per unit of electricity consumed were the fourth highest among EU countries in 2009 (Ecofys, 2011). In the case of wind, tendering for licensing was introduced in 2005, thus promoting cost-efficiency (IEA, 2009), and the feed-in tariff payable to the ensuing new generators was brought down to EUR 75 per megawatt hour (MWh) or below, broadly in line with values in

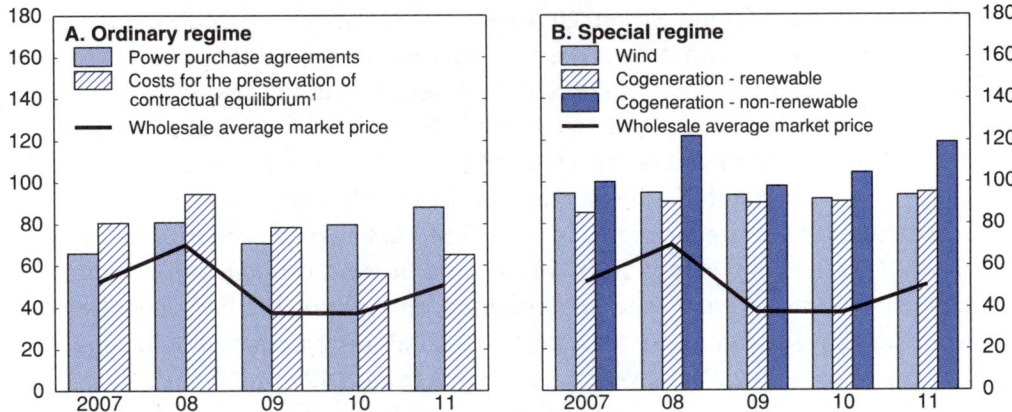

Figure 2.11. **Unit revenue paid to electricity generators**
Annual average, euros per megawatt hour

1. This covers fixed and variable costs and therefore depends on the power plants' utilisation (e.g. unit revenue tends to decrease in rainy years). Data in 2007 refer only to the second half of the year.
Source: Energy Services Regulatory Authority.

StatLink ⟶ http://dx.doi.org/10.1787/888932670218

other EU countries (OECD, 2011). However, around 80% of the existing wind capacity is still being paid under older tariffs, above EUR 90/MWh. Support goes far beyond wind farms. Cogeneration production, largely in the industrial sector, has also increased over the last years with the introduction of a significant feed-in tariff (Figure 2.11), indexed to oil prices, payable on all electricity produced (IEA, 2008a). As regards fossil-fuel power and large hydro plants, most benefit from financial mechanisms which guarantee a pre-established rate of return. Their effective rates of return are complex to estimate precisely but are currently clearly above their average cost of capital (Portuguese Government, 2012). Other generators have received payments for availability which have entailed a deadweight loss as they were granted as an incentive to investment but applied to already existing plants.

All costs of generation support are supposed to be passed on to prices paid by end-consumers of electricity, but so far only part of the costs has. In 2012, costs with subsidies to electricity generators passed on to end-users will account for 14% of the average electric bill and 64% of total passed-on policy costs (Figure 2.12). The allocation of

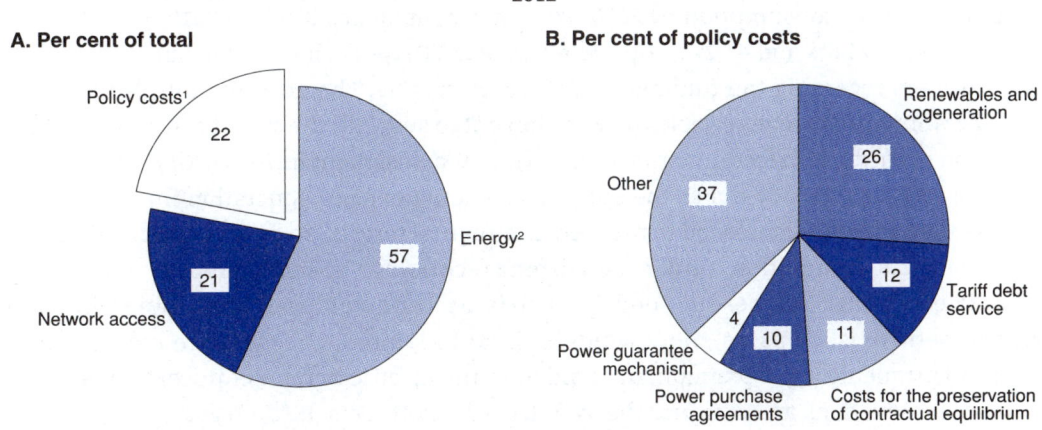

Figure 2.12. **Average electricity price structure**
2012

1. Support to generators is 14% of total and other policy costs are 8%.
2. Energy and commercialisation costs of the supplier (market determined).
Source: Energy Services Regulatory Authority.

StatLink ⟶ http://dx.doi.org/10.1787/888932670237

these costs differs among consumers, falling more on households than on industrial users (ERSE, 2012), which helps explain the internationally very high electricity prices faced by households. Still, prices for industry in 2011 were already above the OECD Europe average, according to preliminary estimates. As the government decided on several occasions not to fully transmit to prices the costs of support to generators, it has created a liability to be paid in the future by all end-users of electricity. This tariff debt reached EUR 1.8 billion at end-2011 (about 1% of GDP) and is expected to be close to EUR 3 billion at end-2012 (ERSE, 2011). This crowds out credit to other sectors, as the debt has been securitised with banks (i.e. the entitlement to future payments is transferred to banks in exchange for an upfront payment to the electricity companies), and should be paid through future increases in electricity prices. If no reforms were implemented, eliminating the tariff debt by 2020, as the authorities have committed to under the EU-IMF programme, would require that electricity prices grow by 2.8% per year in real terms from 2012 to 2020.

Ensuring that electricity generation support is made cost-effective

The authorities must ensure that electricity generation support is made cost-effective and costs are fully passed on to all consumers. This requires reducing excessive supports to both wind farms and cogeneration, and to fossil-fuel power and large hydro plants. Also, the authorities should avoid cross subsidisation between households and industrial users when allocating support costs. Under the EU-IMF programme commitments, the government announced in May 2012 an intended reduction of overall support costs by around 1% of GDP over the period 2012-20, but some measures are still to be legislated or negotiated with electricity generators. Preliminary estimates suggest that in overall terms the announced support reduction will decrease the real electricity price increases required to eliminate the tariff debt by 2020 by only 20-25%.

In the case of wind farms licensed before the 2005 reform, the authorities should reduce the costs stemming from the much higher tariffs still being paid. As regards cogeneration, the authorities have already legislated a considerable reduction in their future remuneration and committed to curbing fraud. They should also introduce a time limit for feed-in tariffs for renewable cogeneration, as best practices recommend that incentives be transitional and decrease over time to foster technological innovation (IEA, 2008b). As a contribution to EU targets, the government has committed to increasingly ambitious goals for renewables penetration, which currently stand at shares of 31% in gross final energy consumption and 55.3% in electricity consumption by 2020 (Portuguese Republic, 2010). In 2010, actual shares already stood at 24.6% and 41.2%, respectively (DGEG, 2012), placing Portugal among the best EU performers regarding the fulfilment of the 2020 targets. The government plans to keep existing commitments to renewables penetration but to suspend the award of licenses for new generation capacity with feed-in tariffs until further reassessment in 2014 (DGEG, 2012). Given the major progress already made, the authorities should expand generation from renewable sources only to the extent needed to meet environmental targets, so as to minimise short-run economic costs. In addition, under the current technology-specific support scheme, the authorities should phase-out feed-in tariffs as renewables technologies become cost-competitive (such as on-shore wind) or, if still required, choose more market-based support instruments (e.g. a premium in addition to the electricity market price) to incentivise further cost reductions and optimise the overall generation costs (IEA, 2011).

In the case of fossil-fuel power and large hydro plants, the authorities should reduce the rates of return currently being paid to EDP and to generators holding power purchase agreements, aiming at bringing returns closer to their average cost of capital. EDP has already communicated to financial markets that it expects a minor reduction of its returns, but authorities should aim for more ambitious results in the on-going negotiations with generators. In addition, the government has already committed to redesign future payments for availability and suppressed the existing ones. Future payments will include a subsidy to thermal plants for their availability, to be granted only after the end of the EU-IMF programme, and an incentive to investment in new hydroelectric plants.

Promoting greater competition in the energy market

Concerns about only limited competition in both electricity and gas remain. Wholesale and especially retail electricity markets are still highly concentrated. In wholesale markets, although substantial new interconnection capacity has been added between Portugal and Spain, in some months of 2010 and 2011 there was noticeable market splitting resulting in differential prices, usually a higher price in Portugal than Spain. The regulator should monitor if the foreseen expansion of interconnection capacity is enough to reduce congestion and market splitting and ensure that Portugal reaps the full benefits of the joint Iberian electricity market.

Though competition in retail electricity markets will likely increase with the phasing-out of the remaining regulated tariffs, progress may be slow as penetration in the household segment, where EDP is strongest, entails high entry costs (administrative and commercial structures). In this framework, transitory regulated tariffs should be managed so as to ensure that consumers switch to the liberalised market while levelling the playing field for competing suppliers. More generally, the powers of the sector regulator should be further strengthened, namely with the adoption of legislation regarding the imposition of sanctions. Sound regulation is all the more important in the present context of full liberalisation and privatisation of natural monopoly network industries.

Despite steps towards liberalisation, wholesale and retail gas markets remain highly concentrated and prices are high by international comparison. Work on a joint Iberian gas market commenced in 2008 but it has been impeded by high cross-border transmission charges between Portugal and Spain. To encourage greater competition, the Portuguese energy regulator, in tandem with the Spanish energy regulator, should fully implement the recent inter-governmental agreement to reduce the cross-border transmission charges between Portugal and Spain to zero. Moreover, the incumbent, GALP Energia, owns exclusive contract rights to the supply of wholesale pipeline gas from Algeria, which is cheaper than sources available to competitors. The regulator should further require GALP to auction Algerian pipeline gas to other firms with no pre-set minimum price. Previous auctions have failed because the regulator allowed GALP to auction the wholesale gas at a price infinitesimally below the retail one allowing no margin for a competitor.

Reforming the labour market to create jobs and help rebalance the economy

Labour market conditions have deteriorated sharply

Portugal has suffered large-scale job losses since 2008 (close to 9% up to the first quarter of 2012), which have taken total employment back to 1997 levels. Though the construction sector has been hit hardest, shedding around a quarter of its workforce, important losses have also been recorded in services (especially hospitality and trade), manufacturing and the primary sector. The contraction in employment has affected young workers the most, and has fallen exclusively on the low skilled (though job creation for workers with secondary or tertiary education has not been fast enough to prevent a rise in unemployment among these groups). Unlike in most other countries (de Serres et al., 2012), average hours worked have remained broadly stable, placing the full burden of accommodating lower total hours on employment.

Job losses have led to soaring unemployment, but also inactivity and emigration. The unemployment rate, at 14.9% in the first quarter of 2012, has risen by more than two thirds since 2008, for both cyclical and structural reasons (see below). Increases have been stronger among those with lower or intermediate qualifications and fairly proportional across age groups, though the 15-24 cohort has been somewhat more penalised than others and unemployment rates remain strongly decreasing with age. The fall in the labour force has come from those under 35 and the low-skilled. Participation rates have decreased markedly in the 15-24 age range, partly as a result of a return to school. Among those aged 25-34, however, participation rates have edged up marginally, which cannot be explained by population ageing alone and suggests growing emigration flows. Though up-to-date statistical indicators are scarce, there is abundant anecdotal evidence of both skilled and unskilled workers moving abroad, often to Portuguese speaking countries like Brazil or Angola.

The financial and sovereign debt crises have exacerbated long-standing weaknesses of the Portuguese labour market, rooted in defective institutional settings in employment protection legislation, unemployment benefits, active labour market policies, and wage setting mechanisms. The unemployment rate had been increasing long before the crisis, with long-term unemployment accounting for about half of the total. Though overall employment barely changed in 2001-07, there were important shifts towards non-tradable sectors, with manufacturing losing more weight in the total than in other countries (2.9 percentage points *versus* 1.9 for the EU average). Labour market reforms are essential to help rebalance the economy and return to growth, by fostering labour reallocation from non-tradable to tradable sectors and getting the unemployed back to work. Building on recent progress, achieved with broad political support, reforms should continue to be pursued without delay, to stave off the threats to social cohesion and potential growth posed by high and persistent unemployment and a shrinking labour force.

Reforms in wage setting and lower non-wage labour costs can help create jobs

Shortcomings in wage setting mechanisms help to explain the difficulty in regaining competitiveness and the sharp rise in joblessness, especially among the low skilled. Wage bargaining mainly takes place at the sectoral level (Marques et al., 2009), where collective agreements are often negotiated between trade unions (sole owners of the right to negotiate on the workers' side) and employers' associations (generally dominated by the largest firms), each of which accounting for only a modest share of total sectoral employment. These agreements are then administratively extended to whole industries (through the *portarias de extensão*), setting a myriad of wage floors across the economy and giving extra clout to those sitting at the negotiations table.

Administrative extension effectively stifles firm-level bargaining, thus contributing to hindering competition in labour and product markets (Bassanini and Duval, 2006; Traxler et al., 2001). Individual companies can only opt out of a sectoral agreement through a firm-level one, but unless the latter is more favourable to workers, trade unions (or, in companies with a workforce of at least 500, works councils under delegation of unions) will have little incentive to negotiate. In international comparison, Portugal ranks high in the degree of administrative extension (Visser, 2011), which tends to reduce the sensitivity of wages to unemployment and thus raise unemployment persistence (de Serres et al., 2012).

Upward pressures on wages were compounded by very strong minimum wage increases in 2007-10 (5.3% per year on average), followed by a further 2.1% rise in 2011. Though contributing to a decrease in inequality in the lower half of the wage distribution, those hikes have led to job losses for the low skilled, especially among youths and in manufacturing (Centeno et al., 2011). Further, the share of minimum-wage earners in total employees rose from around 8% in 2006 to over 12% in 2010. For low-skilled workers, this is likely to have led to a major compression of the wage cushion (the difference between actual wages and collectively bargained wages), making firms lose an important degree of freedom in alleviating the constraints stemming from collective bargaining (Marques et al., 2009).

In welcome steps, the authorities have halted further minimum wage increases and taken measures to promote firm-level bargaining, by lowering the threshold for delegation of unions to works councils from 500 to 150 workers and allowing that sectoral agreements leave the negotiation of certain matters, including wages, to the level of individual firms. Administrative extension was to be frozen until clear criteria for extension have been defined and, in preparing these, the authorities have committed not to extend any collective agreement subscribed to by employers' associations representing less than 50% of workers in a sector and, when that threshold is reached, to take account of the implications on competitiveness when deciding on extension. However, in May 2012 some pending requests for extension not complying with the 50% threshold were accepted, though with some postponement of the associated wage increases. While at a minimum the authorities need to keep their commitments regarding thresholds for extending collective agreements, they should go further and abolish administrative extension altogether. The latter would in itself promote firm-level bargaining, which could also be fostered by providing technical assistance to small firms so as to reduce bargaining transaction costs. Further, the minimum wage should be kept unchanged until there are clear signs of labour market recovery for low-skilled workers.

Recovering competitiveness through non-wage channels helps to smooth short run adjustment costs and the associated employment losses. Instead of a fiscal devaluation tax reform, recommended in the previous *Survey* (OECD, 2010a) and initially foreseen under the EU-IMF financial assistance programme, the authorities have opted (in the context of the recent Labour Code reform) for an increase in working time of up to seven days per year (suppression of four bank holidays and of the up to three extra days of annual leave granted in case of no or few absences), to be implemented in 2013. Other Labour Code changes helping to reduce unit labour costs include more flexible working time arrangements (bank of hours), which decrease the need for overtime, and additional measures to reduce its cost. While these working time reforms should facilitate future adjustment to downturns through hours rather than labour shedding, and be more effective than fiscal devaluation in bringing about lower long run unit labour costs, short-run impacts on employment could be fairly muted. Varejão (2004) analyses an opposite policy decision (the 1996 decrease from 44 to 40 maximum weekly hours) and finds a very modest adverse impact on employment.

Reducing the labour tax wedge on low-wage workers can yield sizeable employment gains, while implying much smaller fiscal costs than a general cut in social contributions. There is evidence that lower tax wedges decrease unemployment (de Serres et al., 2012), and that this decrease could materialise relatively quickly, especially for young people

(OECD, 2012), in contrast with the more muted short-run benefits from other labour market reforms. Potential employment gains from lowering tax wedges are also maximised by the high wage elasticities of labour demand in Portugal (Marques et al., 2009) and by past minimum wage hikes (which took the minimum-to-median wage ratio from 51 to 56% in 2006-10, against an average of 48% across 22 OECD countries in the latter year). As wages in tradable sectors tend to lie below the Portuguese average (OECD, 2010a), targeting a social contributions cut on those earning less than a certain threshold could also yield short-run gains in external competitiveness. Narrower targeting (e.g. temporary cuts requiring net employment gains at firm level, such as those recently introduced under the *Impulso Jovem* programme, targeted at long-term unemployed aged 18-30) implies lower fiscal costs and deadweight losses. However, it tends to be harder to monitor and administer, less effective in terms of employment (job creation could be deterred by the limited duration of the subsidy, or have a similar limited duration), and more likely to distort competition between firms (different job subsidies to otherwise similar firms based on the timing of hiring). The authorities should introduce an open-ended cut in employers' social contributions on low-wage workers, to the extent that compensating measures can ensure that fiscal targets are met.

Recent increases in the level and coverage of the VAT standard rate make it more challenging to cut social contributions while ensuring budget neutrality through compensating measures. It is indeed crucial that any eventual reduction in social contributions does not endanger fiscal targets. However, property taxes could offer some room for manoeuvre. Despite a large housing stock (Figure 2.9), their share in GDP has long been low (1.1% in 2009, against 1.8% for the OECD as a whole), and will remain below-average even once their expected contribution to budget consolidation in 2013 (around 0.15% of GDP) is pencilled in. Revenues from recurrent taxes on immovable property, which accrue to municipalities, are set to increase beyond 2013 (as the higher tax liability stemming from the updated property taxable values will be phased in gradually), and could free central government resources if transfers to local government are concomitantly reduced. In addition, targeting the cut on low-wage workers only (as opposed to a system of progressive rates, simulated in Bank of Portugal et al., 2011) would significantly reduce potential budget costs, though it would also require that the authorities smooth the discontinuity in marginal rates around the threshold, to minimise distortions to the wage distribution, and tackle through stepped up monitoring and sanctions the increased incentive for under-declaration of earnings.

Further reducing segmentation is key to improved labour market performance

High employment protection on regular contracts and the ensuing labour market segmentation lower the sensitivity of wages to unemployment (de Serres et al., 2012) and harm firm performance and productivity growth in different ways. The mobility and reallocation of insiders is hindered, whereas outsiders are caught in a vicious circle of high job rotation and underinvestment in human capital (Centeno and Novo, 2012). The 2009 Labour Code reform, which mainly focussed on reducing procedural inconveniences and notice periods for dismissals, still left Portugal with the highest protection for regular workers in the OECD (Figure 2.13), and with one of the largest gaps in protection between open-ended and temporary contracts.

A new round of Labour Code reforms, started in 2011 and further pursued in 2012, has tackled the more thorny issues of severance pay and causes for dismissal, taking Portugal closer to the OECD average. Individual dismissals grounded on job redundancy no longer

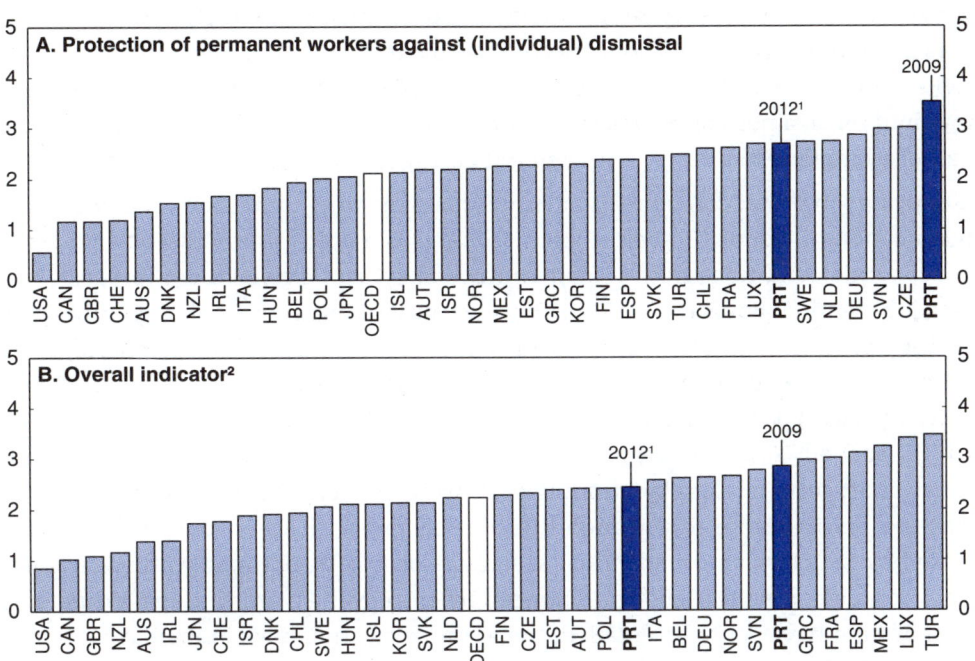

Figure 2.13. **Strictness of employment protection legislation**
Scale from 0 (least stringent) to 6 (most restrictive), 2008

1. Based on changes to the Labour Code due to come into force in August 2012.
2. Weighted average of three sub-indices: protection of permanent workers against (individual) dismissal, regulation on temporary forms of employment and specific requirements for collective dismissal.
Source: OECD (2012), "Employment Protection Legislation", *OECD Employment and Labour Market Statistics* (database), July.
StatLink ⟶ http://dx.doi.org/10.1787/888932670256

need to follow a pre-defined seniority order, while those grounded on worker capability become possible in a wider range of circumstances (for instance, new technologies or other changes to the job are no longer a necessary condition) and the employer no longer needs to attempt a transfer to a possible suitable position. Severance pay has been reduced from 30 to 20 days per year of tenure, with a 12-month ceiling instead of a 3-month floor (while preserving accrued-to-date entitlements, as discussed below), which is still high by international standards.

Despite these efforts, labour market rigidity and segmentation remain above the OECD average, and by actually more than suggested in Figure 2.13, since significant recent reforms in other southern European countries, such as Spain and Italy, have not yet been factored in. The authorities should therefore further reduce severance pay, as envisaged under the financial assistance programme, and do more to tackle duality. A step forward would be to increase the trial period for open-ended contracts (currently 90 days for most workers), though an excessively long duration would risk making open-ended contracts being used as temporary ones. To avoid excessively protracted temporary jobs, the authorities should also ensure that the extension of the maximum number and cumulated duration of successive fixed-term contracts, enacted in January 2012, expires as planned at end-2014 and is not renewed.

Duality also stems from the procedural costs of dismissing permanent workers (Centeno and Novo, 2012), especially when litigation is involved, as court decisions are slow and not always uniform across territorial jurisdictions. Further, it remains to be seen how courts will deal with some of the new legal provisions, such as the firms' obligation, in dismissals for job redundancy, to define relevant and non-discriminatory criteria to replace the previous seniority rule. To reduce delays and uncertainty, which penalise firms and workers alike, the authorities should, as envisaged, introduce binding arbitration (entered into on a voluntary basis) as an alternative to the judicial system in cases of dismissals. In the medium term, a possibility deserving further examination would be to abolish duality altogether by moving to a single employment contract (a flexible open-ended contract).

Reducing job protection on regular contracts takes time to yield productivity gains, as the reallocation of workers to better job matchings is a gradual process, and under harsh macroeconomic conditions may actually induce short-run employment losses, if lay-offs outpace job creation (Bouis et al., 2012). The government has chosen to only fully apply the reduction in severance payments to new hires, while existing contracts preserve entitlements accrued under the old rules until 31 October 2012, and accumulate thereafter at the new (slower) pace if and only if the 12-month ceiling has not been reached, and only until it is reached. This has the advantage of stimulating job creation while helping to minimise short-term job loss by avoiding that firing suddenly becomes cheaper. However, it creates a disincentive to the mobility of workers with long tenure. This could be addressed by the creation of individual severance accounts, portable when changing jobs and paid from a compensation fund financed by employers' contributions. While plans to set up that fund have yet to be detailed, the authorities should avoid increasing non-wage labour costs in the current macroeconomic conditions, which could imply postponing the introduction of the scheme.

Active and passive labour market policies need further reform and integration

The unemployment benefit system has long raised concerns both as regards labour market performance and social equity. Internationally high replacement rates for older workers (OECD, 2010a), essentially driven by benefit duration strongly increasing with age, help to explain high long-term unemployment among those workers (Addison and Portugal, 2008) and may raise reservation wages (Marques et al., 2009). Further, tight eligibility requirements, such as long contributory periods for employees and the exclusion of the self-employed, have led to a below-average coverage of unemployment benefits, made worse by the withdrawal of 2009/10 temporary measures to ease access and extend duration (Figure 2.14). Unsurprisingly, coverage ratios increase with age (from 8.5% for 15-24 year-olds and 30% in the 25-34 age range to 71.4% for those over 45, 2011 data), reflecting age-dependent benefit duration and, above all, that those on the fringes of the labour market (e.g. with short temporary contracts or *de facto* employees forced to be formally self-employed) are mostly young workers. Limited benefit coverage of the latter is all the more worrying as there is some indication that austerity measures in Portugal could be imposing a heavy burden on poor households with children (Callan et al., 2011).

The 2012 reform of unemployment benefits goes some way towards addressing the concerns above, but benefit duration remains heavily age-dependent. Eligibility has been expanded by lowering the minimum required contributory period for unemployment insurance from 15 to 12 months, with effect from 1 July, and by extending benefit entitlement to self-employed workers who get at least 80% of their annual income from a single entity (often *de facto* employees), though in this case a number of additional requirements will defer any practical application until 2013. Further, in 2012, as in 2010, a

Figure 2.14. **Ratio of unemployment benefit recipients to the number of unemployed**[1]

2010[2]

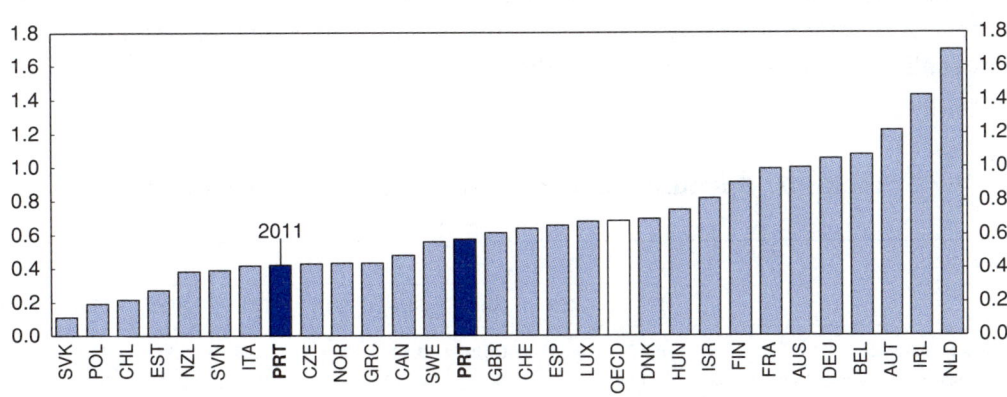

1. Recipients of programmes classified as unemployment insurance or unemployment assistance divided by Labour Force Survey unemployment. Due to institutional specificities, the programme classification cannot ensure perfect cross-country comparability. The ratio for Portugal was 0.57 in 2010 which dropped to 0.42 in 2011 (0.46 adjusting for the break in series at end 2010). The OECD aggregate is an unweighted average of data shown.
2. 2008 for Norway.

Source: OECD (2012), *OECD Employment and Labour Market Statistics* (database), July and Ministry of Solidarity and Social Security.

StatLink ⏵ http://dx.doi.org/10.1787/888932670275

10% increase in unemployment insurance will be granted to lone parents or unemployed couples with children. To tackle disincentives to work, the ceiling on unemployment insurance has been lowered by one sixth, a 10% benefit reduction applies after six months, and older workers will see larger cuts in unemployment insurance duration. However, for those 40 and over, the cuts in duration will be partly compensated by longer provision of unemployment assistance (*subsídio social de desemprego* – a smaller, means-tested benefit paid when entitlement to unemployment insurance ends), so that total benefit duration decreases only slightly. Furthermore, current benefit recipients are largely unaffected, and current workers will be entitled to benefits under the old rules in their first post-reform unemployment spell, compounding the risk that the reform will do little to tackle high long-term unemployment among older workers. Benefit duration should therefore be revisited and made age-independent, with much faster phasing-in provisions. The authorities should also assess whether changes to eligibility prove effective in improving benefit coverage, especially for young workers.

Job search assistance, generally a cost-effective active labour market policy (Card et al., 2010), has substantial room for improvement in Portugal. The few existing formal studies point to only a modest impact on unemployment duration (Centeno et al., 2009), and the share in total hiring of public employment service (PES) vacancy registration and placements (around 23 and 13% in the mid-2000s, respectively) are on the low side by international standards (Duell et al., 2010, Table 3.4). Reasons include poor targeting of resources on those jobseekers most in need of assistance, shortcomings in job search monitoring and sanctions for non-compliance (further discussed below), low outreach to employers, an inefficient use of available information when matching jobseekers to posted vacancies, and limited performance assessment of PES centres and associated networks (such as the *Gabinetes de Inserção Profissional*, created in 2009). Some of these problems were likely compounded by a lack of resources, as the PES budget and staff have not kept pace with rising unemployment (Table 2.2). In a welcome step, the government has recently launched a programme for PES reform (Box 2.2), with measures to address the above weaknesses and clear deadlines for implementation. The authorities should carefully monitor the programme's impacts to inform further improvements. To foster compliance with deadlines, periodic information on the roll-out of the different measures should be made public.

Table 2.2. **Spending on active labour market programmes**
Per cent of GDP

	Portugal			Other OECD Europe[1]			OECD non-Europe[1]		
	2004	2008	2010	2004	2008	2010	2004	2008	2010
Total active measures	**0.66**	**0.55**	**0.72**	**0.69**	**0.63**	**0.80**	**0.21**	**0.22**	**0.27**
Public employment service and administration	0.14	0.15	0.14	0.17	0.17	0.19	0.08	0.06	0.06
Training	0.28	0.24	0.40	0.18	0.15	0.19	0.07	0.07	0.10
Employment incentives	0.16	0.12	0.10	0.12	0.12	0.16	0.02	0.02	0.02
Direct job creation	0.04	0.02	0.05	0.09	0.07	0.11	0.01	0.04	0.05
Other	0.04	0.02	0.03	0.12	0.13	0.14	0.03	0.03	0.03
Memorandum item									
Unemployment rate (%)	6.7	7.6	10.8	8.3	6.2	9.4	6.3	5.2	6.6

1. Unweighted averages of 19 countries for Other OECD Europe and 9 countries for OECD non-Europe, including some estimates. Countries excluded are Greece, Iceland, Norway, Switzerland and Turkey.
Source: OECD (2012), *OECD Employment and Labour Market Statistics* and *OECD Economic Outlook: Statistics and Projections* (databases), July.

Box 2.2. **The Programme for PES Reform**

In February 2012, the authorities announced an integrated set of measures to make job search assistance more effective, the *Programa de Relançamento do Serviço Público de Emprego*. This programme aims at increasing public employment service (PES) placements by 50% and PES vacancy registrations by 20% until end-2013, *inter alia* through:

- Providing job search training within two weeks of jobseeker registration, closer interaction with jobseekers and the use of profiling tools to identify those at greatest risk of long-term unemployment.
- More effective procedures in collecting and disseminating vacancies, including the promotion of partnerships with employer associations.
- Greater cooperation with temporary work and private placement agencies.
- Upgrading information technology systems to allow more interactions through internet and a better jobseeker-vacancy matching.
- Better linkages between active and passive measures, such as steps to curb fraud in proving compliance with job search requirements.
- Streamlining of active labour market programme offers and an assessment of their effectiveness.
- Restructuring of the PES agencies network and systematic assessment of their performance.

Job search and availability requirements, underpinned by systematic monitoring and credible sanctions, are important criteria for unemployment benefits eligibility, as they often lead to higher outflows from joblessness and shorter unemployment duration (Johnson and Klepinger, 1994; Graversen and van Ours, 2008). According to the letter of relevant rules, Portugal has the highest overall strictness of benefit eligibility among 36 OECD or EU countries (Venn, 2012), with one sole area of leniency (no job search requirements during participation in active labour market programmes [ALMP]). However, monitoring and sanctions in practice appear far less rigorous. Job search proof must be provided every fortnight but minimum standards are often undemanding (*e.g.* one action per week among a large menu of valid steps, like applying to vacancies, attending interviews or sending out spontaneous job applications). Further, few unemployment benefit recipients actually receive sanctions, which may be partly explained by the severity of the penalties itself (benefit is permanently lost, rather than temporarily reduced or suspended). In 2011, only 1.7% saw their job centre registration and benefit entitlement cancelled, a fairly low figure in international comparison (Gray, 2003). Job search monitoring should be stepped up, with search requirements made more demanding and extended to ALMP participants, and effective sanction enforcement. To support the latter, benefit sanctions should be made less stringent (for instance, a temporary reduction could replace outright cancellation).

With high unemployment, targeted job subsidies may be needed to keep job search requirements credible (OECD, 2010b) and to help vulnerable jobseekers get some employment experience, even though new jobs may last only for the duration of the subsidy (Centeno and Novo, 2012). In this vein, the authorities have launched *Estímulo 2012*, a scheme requiring net employment creation and targeted at those unemployed for at least six months, where employers must provide relevant training and receive for six months a subsidy of up to 60% of the salary. The above mentioned temporary cuts in employers' social contributions under *Impulso Jovem* should also be of value on this count. To further stimulate job search, the authorities have also made it possible to partially cumulate unemployment benefits and a wage. Benefit recipients who accept a full-time job paying less than the benefit amount will remain entitled to half of the benefit for six months, and to a quarter for the following six months (subject to ceilings). To increase targeting while maximising the incentive to taking up work early in the unemployment spell, this re-employment bonus is not available either in the initial or in the final six months of the benefit entitlement period. The scheme also includes provisions to prevent opportunistic behaviour by employers and employees through collusive layoffs followed by rehiring.

Programmes involving training, subsidised internships or direct job creation are generally expensive, and were substantially expanded in 2008-10 (Table 2.2). However, the very few existing evaluation studies cast doubts on their effectiveness. As often in other countries, participation in job creation schemes (*medidas ocupacionais*) was found not to increase the chances of finding a non-subsidised job (Nunes, 2007). Internships are useful in helping young people get a foothold in the labour market, and ambitious new initiatives in the area, like *Passaporte Emprego* (a strand of *Impulso Jovem*), are being launched, aiming to provide a work experience and training to around 50 000 young people who have been unemployed for at least four months. Too generous subsidies for receiving firms, as was arguably the case in the past, could nonetheless entail deadweight losses by displacing unsubsidised hiring. The authorities have commissioned a systematic evaluation of how effective different measures are in fostering exit from unemployment (see Dias and

Varejão, 2011, for a progress report), and should use its findings to carefully target programmes on specific groups of jobseekers. They should also remove the current general exemption from job search requirements during participation in ALMP, as planned, and design programmes so as to leave time for search. This approach is being pursued under the new *Vida Ativa* programme, which aims at providing part-time training early in the unemployment spell.

> **Box 2.3. Summary of recommendations to rebalance the economy and return to growth**
>
> **Unwinding macro-financial imbalances while avoiding a credit crunch**
>
> - Remove barriers to credit reallocation by tackling incentives to investment in sheltered sectors and "ever-greening" of problematic loans.
> - In bank recapitalisation operations, ensure that the potential costs to taxpayers and the final beneficiaries of the funds are fully transparent.
> - Pay special attention to the financing conditions of small and medium-sized enterprises. To make firms more reliant on equity and less on debt, alleviate the debt bias embedded in the tax system, for instance by limiting deductibility of interest payments and using the increase in revenues to reduce the corporate tax rate.
> - Ensure that the pace of convergence towards the indicative target for the loan-to-deposit ratio does not thwart economic activity.
>
> **Removing distortions to capital allocation**
>
> - Ensure that the new eviction procedures effectively decrease the eviction time of non-complying tenants in order to increase the supply of rental housing. Foster urban rehabilitation by cutting red tape and focusing existing financial incentives on dwellings for rental.
> - Reduce the reliance on the real estate transaction tax by levying it only on the initial transactions of property. In a second step, consider replacing it by value-added tax.
> - Ensure that electricity generation support is made cost-effective and costs are fully passed on to all consumers. This requires further reducing excessive supports to both wind farms and cogeneration, and to fossil-fuel power and large hydro plants.
> - Given the major progress already made, further expand generation from renewable sources only to the extent needed to meet environmental targets, so as to minimise short-run economic costs. In addition, as renewable technologies become cost-competitive, phase-out feed-in tariffs or, if still justified, choose more market-based support instruments.
> - Promote greater competition in the energy sector by managing the regulated electricity tariffs phasing-out to ensure that consumers switch to the liberalised retail market and entry by new players takes place. In gas markets, implement the agreement with Spain to lower cross-border transmission charges to zero.
>
> **Reforming the labour market**
>
> - Continue to tackle labour market rigidity and segmentation by further reducing severance pay and introducing binding arbitration in conflicts over dismissals.
> - Further promote firm-level wage bargaining by abolishing administrative extension of collective agreements.

> **Box 2.3. Summary of recommendations to rebalance the economy and return to growth** *(cont.)*
>
> - To avoid increasing non-wage labour costs in the short run, delay the creation of a compensation fund to finance portable individual severance accounts.
> - Make unemployment benefit duration not age dependent, and ensure that changes to eligibility prove effective in improving benefit coverage, especially for young workers.
> - Step up job search assistance and monitoring, with search requirements made more demanding and extended to active labour market programmes participants, and effective sanction enforcement. To support the latter, make benefit sanctions less stringent.
> - Use training and related programmes selectively, so as to maximise employability gains.
> - To improve employment prospects for low-skilled workers and ease labour cost adjustment, reduce employers' social contributions on low-wage workers, to the extent that compensating measures can ensure that fiscal targets are met.

Bibliography

Addison, J.T. and P. Portugal (2008), "How do Different Entitlements to Unemployment Benefits Affect the Transitions from Unemployment into Employment?", *Economics Letters*, Vol. 101, No. 3, Elsevier.

AECOPS (Associação de Empresas de Construção e Obras Públicas e Serviços) (2009), *O Mercado da Reabilitação – Enquadramento, Relevância e Perspectivas*.

Ahrend, R. and A. Goujard (2012), "International Capital Mobility and Financial Fragility – Part 1. Drivers of Systemic Banking Crises: The Role of Bank-Balance-Sheet Contagion and Financial Account Structure", *OECD Economics Department Working Papers*, No. 902, OECD Publishing.

Andrews, D. and A. Caldera Sánchez (2011), "Drivers of Homeownership Rates in Selected OECD Countries", *OECD Economics Department Working Papers*, No. 849, OECD Publishing.

Andrews, D., A. Caldera Sánchez and Å. Johansson (2011), "Housing Markets and Structural Policies in OECD Countries", *OECD Economics Department Working Papers*, No. 836, OECD Publishing.

Bank of Portugal (2011), *Financial Stability Report*, November, Banco de Portugal.

Bank of Portugal et al. (2011), *Desvalorização Fiscal – Relatório*, July, Banco de Portugal, Ministério das Finanças, Ministério da Economia e do Emprego, Ministério da Solidariedade e da Segurança Social.

Bassanini, A. and R. Duval (2006), "Employment Patterns in OECD Countries: Reassessing the Role of Policies and Institutions", *OECD Social, Employment and Migration Working Papers*, No. 35, OECD Publishing.

Beck, T., A. Demirgüç-Kunt and R. Levine (2000), "A New Database on Financial Development and Structure", *World Bank Economic Review*, Vol. 14, No. 3. Updated November 2010.

Blanchard, O. (2007), "Adjustment Within the Euro. The Difficult Case of Portugal", *Portuguese Economic Journal*, Vol. 6, No. 1, Springer.

Bouis, R., O. Causa, L. Demmou, R. Duval and A. Zdzienicka (2012), "The Short-Term Effects of Structural Reforms: An Empirical Analysis", *OECD Economics Department Working Papers*, No. 949, OECD Publishing.

Caldera Sánchez, A. and D. Andrews (2011), "To Move or Not to Move: What Drives Residential Mobility Rates in the OECD?", *OECD Economics Department Working Papers*, No. 846, OECD Publishing.

Callan, T., C. Leventi, H. Levy, M. Matsaganis, A. Paulus and H. Sutherland (2011), "The Distributional Effects of Austerity Measures: A Comparison of Six Countries", *Research Note*, No. 2, Social Situation Observatory, European Commission.

Card, D., J. Kluve and A. Weber (2010), "Active Labour Market Policy Evaluations: A Meta-Analysis", *The Economic Journal*, Vol. 120, No. 548, Royal Economic Society.

Centeno, L., M. Centeno and A.A. Novo (2009), "Evaluating Job-Search Programs for Old and Young Individuals: Heterogeneous Impact on Unemployment Duration", *Labour Economics*, Vol. 16, No. 1, Elsevier.

Centeno, M., C. Duarte and A.A. Novo (2011), "The Impact of the Minimum Wage on Low-Wage Earners", *Economic Bulletin*, Vol. 17, No. 3, Banco de Portugal.

Centeno, M. and A.A. Novo (2012), "Segmentation", *Economic Bulletin*, Vol. 18, No. 1, Banco de Portugal.

DGEG (Direcção Geral de Energia e Geologia) (2012), Linhas Estratégicas para a Revisão dos Planos Nacionais de Ação para as Energias Renováveis e Eficiência Energética (Versão para Discussão Pública), June.

Dias, M.C. and J. Varejão (2011), *Estudo de Avaliação das Políticas Ativas de Emprego, 1 Relatório de Progresso*, Centro de Economia e Finanças and Faculdade de Economia da Universidade do Porto, December.

Duell, N., D. Grubb, S. Singh and P. Tergeist (2010), "Activation Policies in Japan", *OECD Social, Employment and Migration Working Papers*, No. 113, OECD Publishing.

Ecofys (2011), *Financing Renewable Energy in the European Energy Market*, Final Report for the European Commission, DG Energy, January.

EMF (European Mortgage Federation) (2010), *Study on the Cost of Housing in Europe*.

ERSE (Energy Services Regulatory Authority) (2011), "Tarifas e Preços para a Energia Eléctrica em 2012", *Comunicado*, December, Entidade Reguladora dos Serviços Energéticos.

ERSE (2012), "Composição dos Preços de Electricidade para 2012", *Nota Informativa*, January, Entidade Reguladora dos Serviços Energéticos.

Graversen, B.K. and J.C. van Ours (2008), "Activating Unemployed Workers Works; Experimental Evidence from Denmark", *Economics Letters*, Vol. 100, Elsevier.

Gray, D. (2003), "National Versus Regional Financing and Management of Unemployment and Related Benefits: The Case of Canada", *OECD Social, Employment and Migration Working Papers*, No. 14, OECD Publishing.

IEA (International Energy Agency) (2008a), "Feed-In Tariffs: Making CHP and DCH Viable – Portugal Case Study", International CHP/DHC Collaborative.

IEA (2008b), *Deploying Renewables: Principles for Effective Policies*, International Energy Agency, OECD Publishing.

IEA (2009), *Energy Policies of IEA countries: Portugal 2009 Review*, International Energy Agency, OECD Publishing.

IEA (2011), *Deploying Renewables 2011: Best and Future Policy Practice*, International Energy Agency, OECD Publishing.

IMF (International Monetary Fund) (2009), "The Economics of Bank Restructuring: Understanding the Options", *IMF Staff Position Note*, June.

IMF (2012), *Global Financial Stability Report*, April, International Monetary Fund.

Johnson, T. and D. Klepinger (1994), "Experimental Evidence on Unemployment Insurance Work-Search Policies", *Journal of Human Resources*, Vol. 29, No. 3, University of Wisconsin Press.

Kappeler, A. and M. Nemoz (2010), "Public-Private Partnerships in Europe – Before and During the Recent Financial Crisis", *Economic and Financial Report*, No. 4, European Investment Bank.

Lamo, A., J.J. Perez and L. Schuknecht (2008), "Public and Private Sector Wages. Co-movement and Causality", *Working Paper Series*, No. 963, European Central Bank.

Lopes, J. and J.E. Gata (2005), *A Comparative Overview of the Progress Achieved to Date in the Construction of the EC Internal Energy Market*, Revised Public Version: 9 November, Autoridade da Concorrência (Portugal).

Marques, C.R., F. Martins and P. Portugal (2009), "Price and Wage Setting in Portugal", *The Portuguese Economy in the Context of Economic, Financial and Monetary Integration*, Economics and Research Department, Banco de Portugal.

Merler, S. and J. Pisani-Ferry (2012), *Sudden Stops in the Euro Area*, Bruegel Policy Contribution, No. 2012/06, Breugel.

Ministry of Finance (2011), *Documento de Estratégia Orçamental 2011-2015*, August, Ministério das Finanças.

Nunes, A. (2007), "Microeconometric Studies on Programme Causal Effects – Empirical Evidence from Portuguese Active Labour Market Policy", PhD Dissertation, Universidade de Coimbra.

OECD (2010a), *OECD Economic Surveys: Portugal 2010*, OECD Publishing.

OECD (2010b), *OECD Employment Outlook 2010: Moving Beyond the Jobs Crisis*, OECD Publishing.

OECD (2011), *OECD Environmental Performance Reviews: Portugal 2011*, OECD Publishing.

OECD (2012), *Economic Policy Reforms 2012: Going for Growth*, OECD Publishing.

OTB (Research Institute for the Built Environment) (2010), *Housing Statistics in the European Union*, K. Dol and M. Haffner (eds.), Delft University of Technology, September.

Portuguese Government (2012), "Report with the Scope of Measure 5.15 of the Second Regular Review of the Memorandum of Understanding on Specific Economic Policy Conditionality", internal working document, February, Governo de Portugal.

Portuguese Republic (2010), Plano Nacional de Acção para as Energias Renováveis ao Abrigo da Directiva 2009/28/CE, República Portuguesa.

Serres, A. de, F. Murtin and C. de la Maisonneuve (2012), "Tackling Unemployment in a Weak Post-Crisis Recovery: Policies to Facilitate the Return to Work", *OECD Economics Department Working Papers*, OECD Publishing, forthcoming.

Traxler, F., S. Blaschke and B. Kittel (2001), *National Labour Relations in Internationalized Markets, A Comparative Study of Institutions, Change, and Performance*, Oxford University Press.

Varejão, J. (2004), "Redução do Tempo de Trabalho e Emprego – Lições da Lei das 40 horas", Proceedings of the 2nd Conference on Portuguese Economic Development in the European Context, Bank of Portugal, Lisbon, 11-12 March.

Venn, D. (2012), "Eligibility Criteria for Unemployment Benefits. Quantitative Indicators for OECD and EU countries", *OECD Social, Employment and Migration Working Papers*, No. 131, OECD Publishing.

Visser, J. (2011), "Data Base on Institutional Characteristics of Trade Unions, Wage Setting, State Intervention and Social Pacts, 1960-2010 (ICTWSS)", Version 3.0, May, Amsterdam Institute for Advanced Labour Studies AIAS, University of Amsterdam.

Glossary

ALMP	Active labour market programme
ANA	*Aeroportos de Portugal* (airport operator)
CoCos	Contingent convertible securities
CP	*Comboios de Portugal* (operator of train services)
EBA	European Banking Authority
ECB	European Central Bank
EDP	*Energias de Portugal* (national electricity company)
EP	*Estradas de Portugal* (national road concessionaire)
EU	European Union
EUR	Euro
FDI	Foreign direct investment
GALP	*GALP Energia* (national gas company)
GDP	Gross domestic product
IMF	International Monetary Fund
MVNO	Mobile virtual network operator
MWh	Megawatt hour
PES	Public employment service
PISA	Programme for International Student Assessment
PPP	Public-private partnership
R&D	Research and development
REFER	*Rede Ferroviária Nacional* (national rail track company)
REN	*Rede Eléctrica Nacional* (national electricity transmission network company)
SME	Small and medium-sized enterprises
SOE	State-owned enterprise
TAP	National airline company
US	United States
UTAO	*Unidade Técnica de Apoio Orçamental* (Parliamentary technical budget support unit)
VAT	Value-added tax
VET	Vocational education and training

ORGANISATION FOR ECONOMIC CO-OPERATION AND DEVELOPMENT

The OECD is a unique forum where governments work together to address the economic, social and environmental challenges of globalisation. The OECD is also at the forefront of efforts to understand and to help governments respond to new developments and concerns, such as corporate governance, the information economy and the challenges of an ageing population. The Organisation provides a setting where governments can compare policy experiences, seek answers to common problems, identify good practice and work to co-ordinate domestic and international policies.

The OECD member countries are: Australia, Austria, Belgium, Canada, Chile, the Czech Republic, Denmark, Estonia, Finland, France, Germany, Greece, Hungary, Iceland, Ireland, Israel, Italy, Japan, Korea, Luxembourg, Mexico, the Netherlands, New Zealand, Norway, Poland, Portugal, the Slovak Republic, Slovenia, Spain, Sweden, Switzerland, Turkey, the United Kingdom and the United States. The European Union takes part in the work of the OECD.

OECD Publishing disseminates widely the results of the Organisation's statistics gathering and research on economic, social and environmental issues, as well as the conventions, guidelines and standards agreed by its members.

OECD PUBLISHING, 2, rue André-Pascal, 75775 PARIS CEDEX 16
(10 2012 15 1 P) ISBN 978-92-64-12798-2 – No. 60183 2012-02